ROUTLEDGE LIBRARY EDITIONS: WW2

Volume 34

TOBRUK 1941

TOBRUK 1941
The Desert Siege

TIMOTHY HALL

Routledge
Taylor & Francis Group

LONDON AND NEW YORK

First published in 1984 by Methuen Australia

This edition first published in 2022
by Routledge
2 Park Square, Milton Park, Abingdon, Oxon OX14 4RN

and by Routledge
605 Third Avenue, New York, NY 10158

Routledge is an imprint of the Taylor & Francis Group, an informa business

© 1984 Timothy Hall

All rights reserved. No part of this book may be reprinted or reproduced or utilised in any form or by any electronic, mechanical, or other means, now known or hereafter invented, including photocopying and recording, or in any information storage or retrieval system, without permission in writing from the publishers.

Trademark notice: Product or corporate names may be trademarks or registered trademarks, and are used only for identification and explanation without intent to infringe.

British Library Cataloguing in Publication Data
A catalogue record for this book is available from the British Library

ISBN: 978-1-03-201217-9 (Set)
ISBN: 978-1-00-319367-8 (Set) (ebk)
ISBN: 978-1-03-207931-8 (Volume 34) (hbk)
ISBN: 978-1-03-207935-6 (Volume 34) (pbk)
ISBN: 978-1-00-321214-0 (Volume 34) (ebk)

DOI: 10.4324/9781003212140

Publisher's Note
The publisher has gone to great lengths to ensure the quality of this reprint but points out that some imperfections in the original copies may be apparent.

Disclaimer
The publisher has made every effort to trace copyright holders and would welcome correspondence from those they have been unable to trace.

TOBRUK 1941

The Desert Siege

Timothy Hall

Methuen Australia

For Tim
With love

Devised and produced by Taylor-Type
Publications (Australia) Pty Ltd
First published in 1984 by
Methuen Australia Pty Ltd
44–50 Waterloo Road, North Ryde 2113

© Timothy Hall 1984

This book is copyright. Apart from
any fair dealing for the purposes
of private study, research, criticism
or review, as permitted under the
Copyright Act, no part may be
reproduced by any process without
written permission. Inquiries should
be addressed to Methuen Australia Pty Ltd.

National Library of Australia
Cataloguing-in-Publication data
Hall, Timothy.
   Tobruk 1941.
   ISBN 0 454 00667 5.
   1. Tobruk, Battles of, 1941–1942.
   2. World War, 1939–1945 — Campaigns —
     Africa, North. I. Title.
940.54'23

Typesetting by Rochester Photosetting
Service, Sydney
Designed by M. D. Camp
Printed in Hong Kong

Contents

Introduction   9

Early Victory   11

The Superb Tactician   26

Retreat and Defence   45

The Fierce Onslaught   60

Security and Prisoners   92

Holding Out   107

Under Siege   123

'Your Magnificent Defence ...'   157

Stalemate   174

Operation Battleaxe   189

Operation Crusader   203

Bibliography   220

Index   221

'The war in Africa is something different. It is simply a question of man against man, eye to eye, blow for blow. Were the battle not so brutal, one could compare it with the romantic idea of jousting among knights.'

> From the diary of a German tank commander.

'The whole Empire is watching your steadfast and spirited defence of this important outpost of Egypt, with gratitude and admiration.'

> Winston Churchill,
> 7 May 1941.

'Immensely big and powerful men, who without question represented an élite formation of the British Empire.'

> General Erwin Rommel, of
> the Australians defending Tobruk.

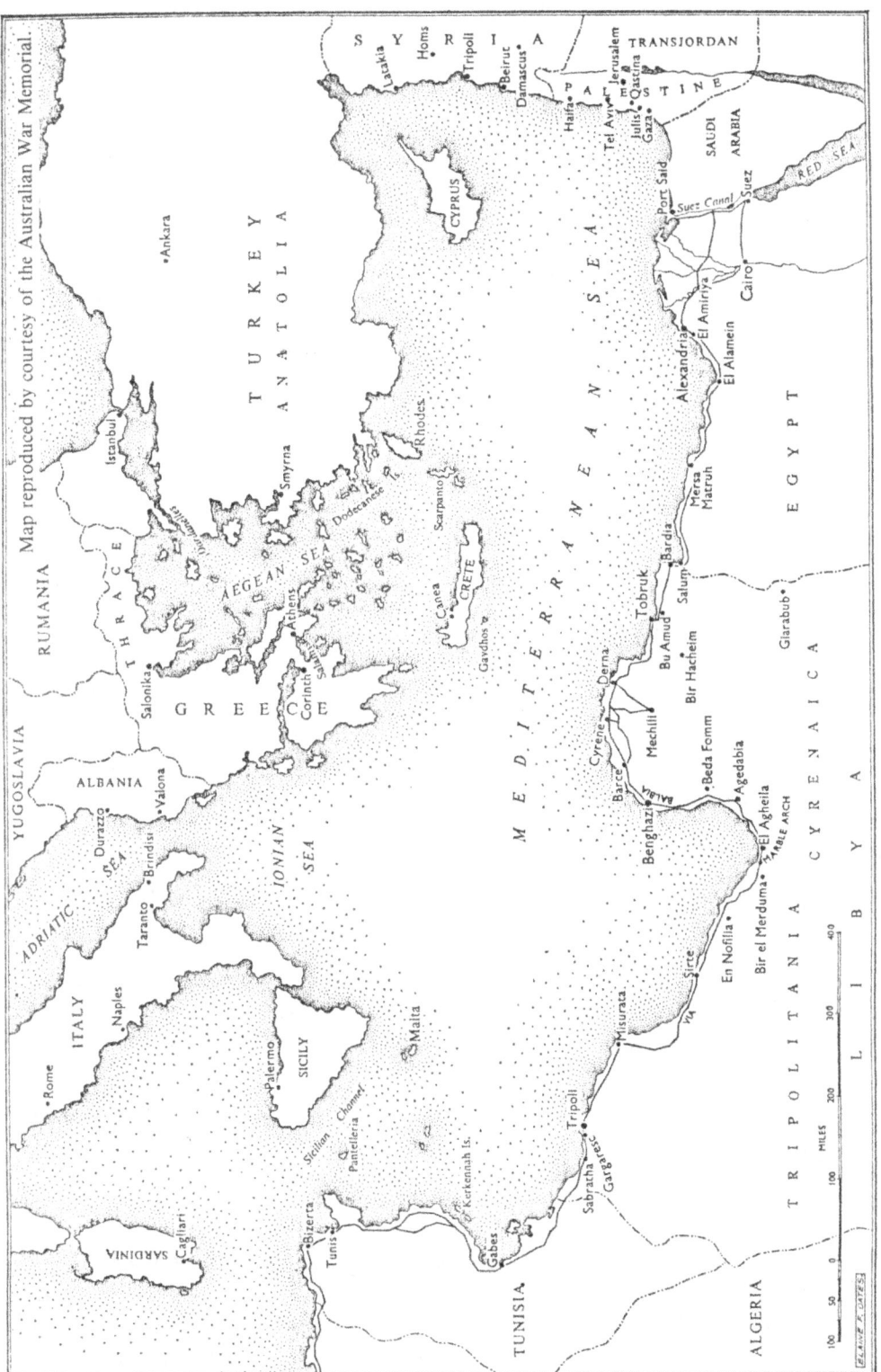

The Eastern Mediterranean

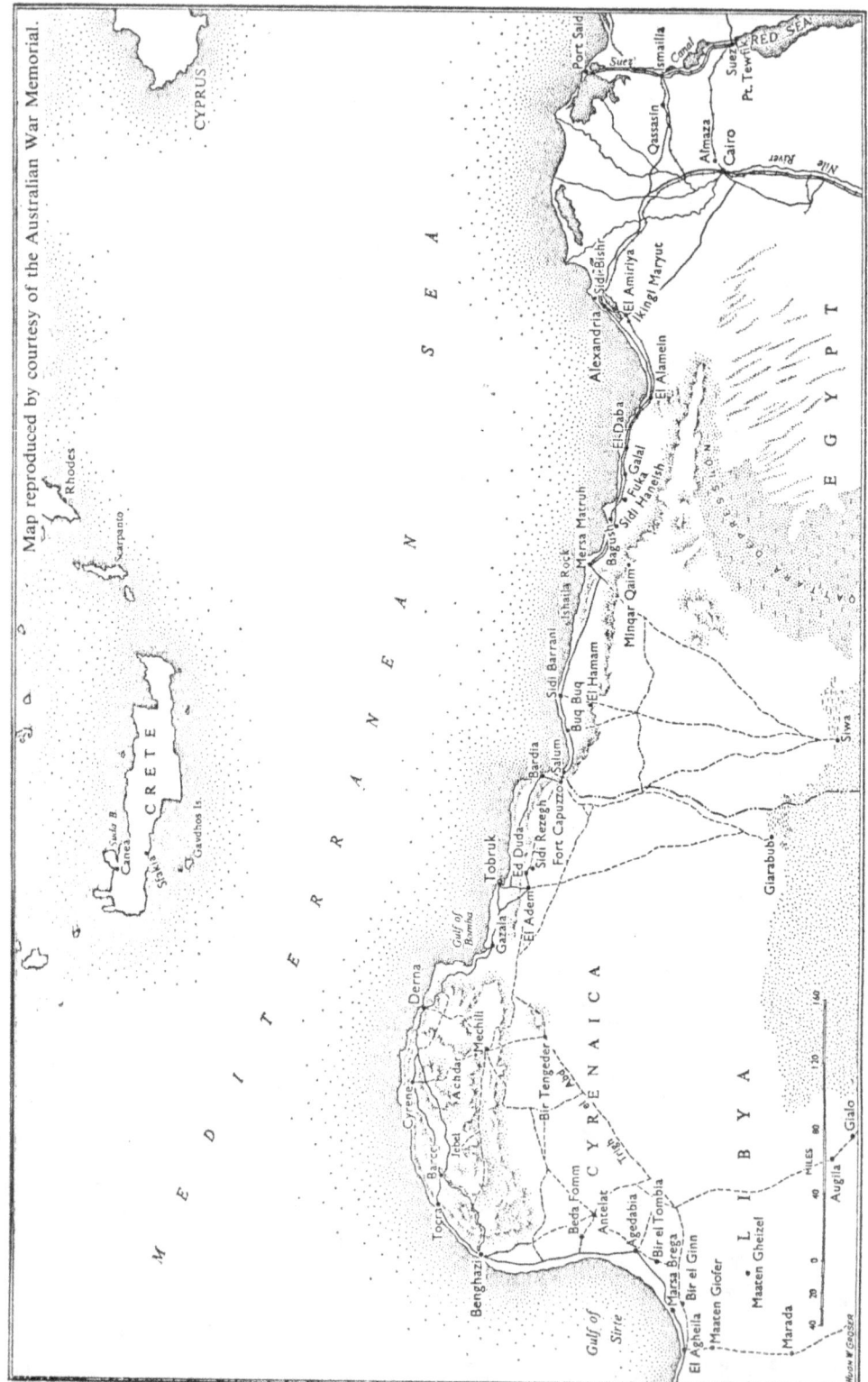

The Western Desert

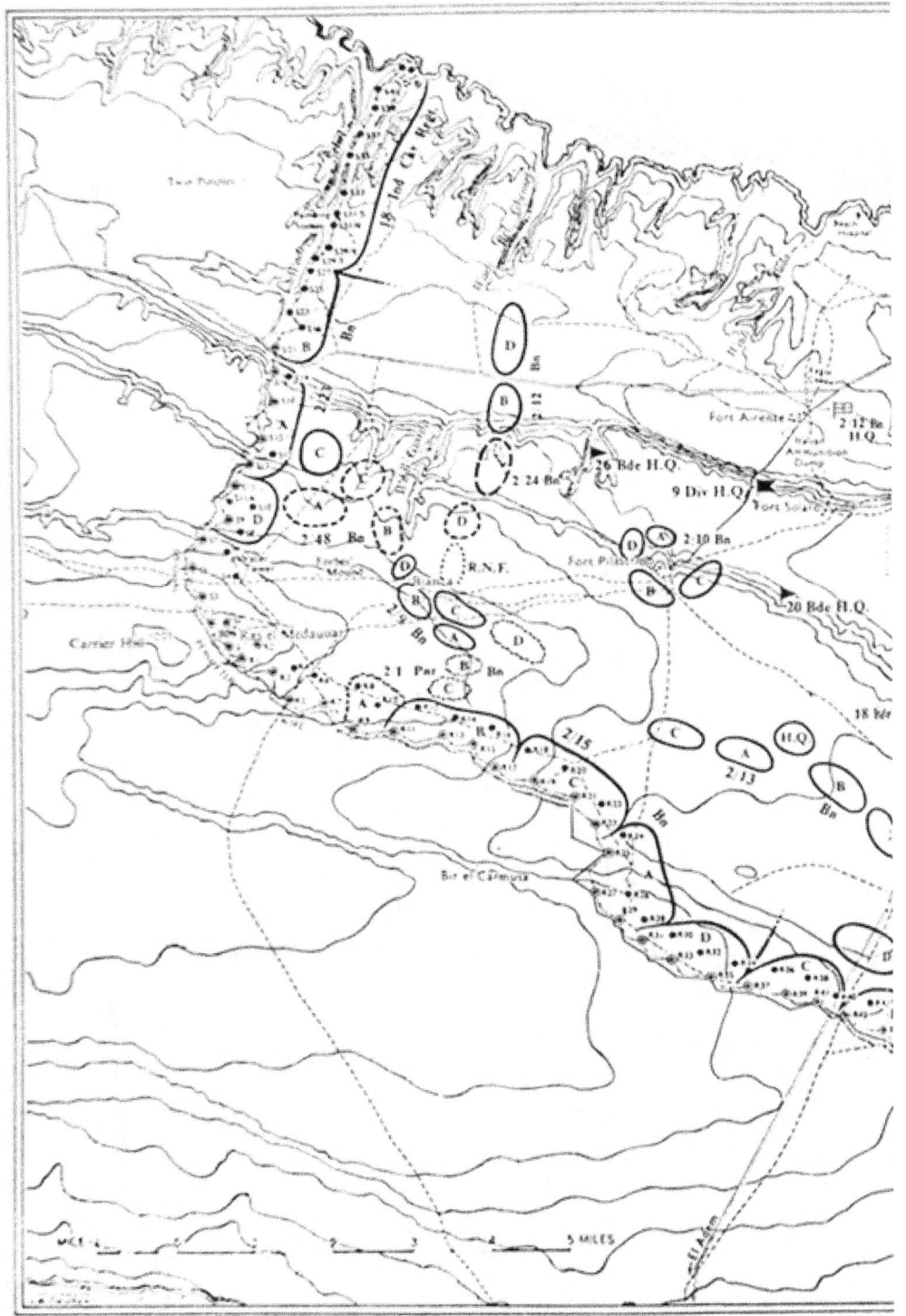

Map reproduced by courtesy of the Australian War Memorial.

Introduction

Siege conjures up many images, usually of men standing their ground against superior odds, prepared to fight to the last rather than surrender. The siege of Tobruk was certainly not in conflict with that picture.

Early in 1941 the Allies, fleeing ignominiously before the forces of the brilliant new German Desert Commander, Erwin Rommel, suddenly turned on their pursuers at the former Italian fortress of Tobruk. There they made their stand. They fought back tooth and claw for nearly eight months and tied up the Axis army so effectively that Rommel was prevented from taking his attack into Egypt and was denied a most vital base in the Eastern Mediterranean.

The men who withstood the siege with such bravery and persistence were largely Australian infantrymen supported by British artillery. The conditions they fought under were appalling, the strain sometimes unbearable.

The Desert War has always been thought of as one of the more 'civilised' campaigns of World War II — a curious word for a struggle of fearsome bloodiness where hand-to-hand fighting with the bayonet was a daily event; where the flame-thrower was frequently used at close range; and where men were forced to lie or crouch all day in shallow trenches, certain only that if they stood up even momentarily in daylight, they would die for their carelessness.

Yet it is not difficult to see how this myth developed. Both sides fought under equally appalling conditions, almost eyeball-to-eyeball on either side of the barbed wire perimeter fence; enduring the flies, the awful heat and dust and dirt, the constant stomach disorders;

wondering if it would ever end and if the miserable patch of sand they were fighting over was worth all the suffering and death.

Germans and Australians alike developed a very strong mutual respect for each other's courage and skill as soldiers; just as Germans and Australians alike shared a healthy and useful contempt for the much despised Italian infantrymen who were almost as much a liability to their German allies as they were cluttering up the fortress when they ran to surrender in their thousands. One of the enduring cameos in the campaign is of German panzer units breaking off an attack on the Australian lines to fire a contemptuous volley at the fast-retreating backs of the Italians as they scurried to the safety of the nearest sand dune as soon as they came under fire.

In no campaign was so strong a link forged between Australians and British fighting together. The catalyst throughout the siege was the Fortress Commander, Australian General Leslie Morshead. He was a difficult man to serve under and to understand, and not all his conduct comfortably stands the glare of close examination; but he remains one of Australia's legendary commanders.

Tobruk was a very proud interlude for Australia in a war that was not going well for the Allies — a war that in fact was going disastrously wrong. The defence of Tobruk was not only marked by great heroism on the part of the Australians, but it was also entirely successful. It was an epic battle and this book is its story, as told by men who served there and by the record that survives in war diaries as well as private diaries kept in the heat of the battle and personal letters.

As always I have been greatly helped by the staff of the Australian War Memorial, although the opinions expressed in the book are my own.

Early Victory

Libya, parched by searing winds and the heat of the great Sahara Desert that makes up nearly ninety-nine per cent of its mass, devoid of almost any protection against an enemy or the elements, has always seemed an unlikely arena for one of the finest military sagas of this century. Yet it was here that the British won the first spectacular victory by either side in the war; and here that men of the Australian army withstood a siege that prompted Robert Menzies to signal 'You are putting up a fight that will live in our history.'

In 1940 Germany and Italy controlled the Mediterranean by force of their superior air power operating from airfields in Sicily and North Africa. The only thorn in their side was little Malta which valiantly refused to surrender and continued to provide the Allies with essential airfields, despite Hitler's confidence that Malta could be subdued.

But this was not sufficient. To be sure that their domination of the Mediterranean was complete, the Axis powers had first to control the three entrances to the sea, Gibraltar in the west, and the Suez Canal and the Dardanelles in the east. And once these were in their grasp, they had to protect them by neutralising the whole of the southern and eastern shores of the Mediterranean which were held by the British.

When Hitler was forced to postpone his plans for invading Britain because of the resistance he encountered there, he turned his attention to bringing the Mediterranean under Axis control. He had already offered German troops to Mussolini for his North African campaign, but the Italians had refused the offer.

Now he proposed three steps for achieving his purpose. With

Franco's help in Spain, Gibraltar would be taken; Syria, which was then French territory, would be overrun with the collaboration of Vichy France; and the Italians in North Africa would push eastwards into Egypt.

His plans, however, started to go awry almost immediately. The first complication was that Franco made it clear that he would not consider taking Spain to war against the British until their collapse was imminent; and Italy, peeved that their ambitions in the Balkans were being constantly thwarted by Germany, invaded Greece without telling Hitler.

The result was infuriating for Hitler. The Italian invasion was a disaster, with the Greeks not only halting them within a few kilometres of the Albanian border but counter-attacking so fiercely that, within a week, Greece occupied a third of Albania which had previously been controlled by Italy. At the same time, British aircraft moved into airfields near Athens where they were within range of the vital oilfields of Romania which were essential to Germany.

These considerations alone should have required the attention of Germany's ground forces. Greece had to be subdued and it was clear that, far from assisting in achieving this, the Italians were a positive liability. Yet on 18 December 1940, Hitler issued his directive that Russia was to be overthrown and that all available troops were to be made available for this purpose.

The Italians were faring no better in North Africa. When Italy declared war against Britain in June 1940, she had an enormous army of nearly 300,000 men in Cyrenaica, the eastern province of Libya, which was already an Italian colony. They were commanded, not too wisely as events were to prove, by Marshal Rodolfo Graziani.

Confronting them (under the command of the British Commander-in-Chief, Middle East, General Sir Archibald Wavell) were just 36,000 British troops who were in Egypt to protect the North African approaches to the Suez Canal. Separating the two sides were 112 km of the Western Desert, with the Italians at Sidi Barrani, and the most forward position of the Allies at Mersa Matruh. Mersa Matruh itself was 200 km east of the Libyan and Cyrenaican frontier.

In September 1940, Wavell had watched as the Italians settled into a chain of widely separated forts and camps and had then waited for the first sign of a move against the Allied troops. Nothing happened. Weeks went by, his own forces were reinforced, notably by three armoured divisions, and the Italians never stirred. He decided to strike first.

On 7 December, he ordered some 30,000 men, under Major-General Richard O'Connor, to advance westwards from Mersa Matruh to attack the Italians. It was the first blow struck in North Africa. He was outnumbered almost three-to-one by more than 80,000 Italians, but whereas the Italians had only 120 tanks at Sidi Barrani, O'Connor had 275, of which 50 were heavily armoured Matildas.

Overnight O'Connor passed through a gap in the chain of forts. He stormed the first, at Nibeiwa, from the rear on the morning of the 9th; he then captured a second fort in the afternoon; and took a third before dusk. The Italians, who did not emerge from the war with a reputation for being among the world's bravest fighters, began to surrender by the thousand.

Their particular horror was of the cold steel of the bayonet, of which the Allies took full advantage. Within minutes of them appearing with bayonets levelled, shouting their war cry, hordes of Italians, yelling and screaming for mercy, took off in the other direction. In a short time, nearly 40,000 of them had been taken, together with 73 tanks and 237 guns, at a price of fewer than 600 men lost on the British side.

By 10 December most of the positions close to Sidi Barrani had been overrun, and on the 11th the reserve tanks made a further enveloping bound to the coast beyond Buq Buq, intercepting a large column of retreating Italians.

Falling back across the frontier into Cyrenaica, the remnants of the Italians from Sidi Barrani withdrew into the fortress of Bardia where they were promptly isolated by O'Connor's tanks. He would have attacked at once but Wavell, ever cautious and calculating, ordered him to wait until the 6th Australian Division arrived to replace an Indian division which had been withdrawn immediately after Sidi Barrani fell.

At last, when the Australians arrived, the order was given for the assault to begin and three days later it was over. The whole Italian garrison surrendered and another 45,000 prisoners were taken.

Wavell had expected Bardia to be harder to take and in a telegram to General Sir John Dill, the Chief of the Imperial General Staff, he lapsed into a string of hunting metaphors that he could never resist using. 'Hunt is still going,' he signalled, 'but first racing burst over. Hounds brought to their noses, huntsmen must cast and second horses badly wanted. It may be necessary to dig this fox.' But the fox needed little digging.

From Bardia the Allies pressed on along the coast road to the next Italian stronghold, the town of Tobruk, with its strongly fortified perimeter and excellent harbour. Tobruk fell on 23/24 January, another 25,000 prisoners joined their compatriots behind barbed wire, and 200 guns and 90 tanks were added to the Allied arsenal.

Tobruk was not the Allies' ultimate objective in Cyrenaica. To complete their conquest of the province, its largest city, the port of Benghazi, had to be captured. After their stunning successes it was not a target that intimidated Wavell or O'Connor, but other events were to forestall them.

Early in January 1941, Churchill had offered increased military aid to Greece and, expecting their speedy acceptance of his offer, had instructed Wavell to prepare without delay for the despatch of tanks and artillery from Egypt to Greece. This would have left O'Connor's forces so depleted, however, that it was doubtful whether he would have had enough strength left to push his advance beyond Tobruk. However, the Greek Premier, Ioannis Metaxas, fearful of provoking Germany, declined Churchill's offer. The operation against Benghazi was allowed to proceed.

The capture of Benghazi was perhaps the most stunning and total victory of the whole North African campaign. Up to this time the strategy had been to encircle the enemy forts and then go in with a fierce attack on the defenders, relying heavily on close combat and the bayonet.

On 3 February 1941, however, O'Connor learned that the Italians were about to abandon Benghazi and to retreat westward down the coast road to El Agheila, where the road from Cyrenaica into the western province of Tripolitania goes through a narrow bottleneck between the sea and the mountains.

He immediately ordered the 7th Armoured Division, from its position at Mechili, south-west of Tobruk, to sweep across the desert at top speed and intercept the Italians by cutting the coast road well to the east of Agheila. At the same time, the Australians would push along the coast road behind the Italians until together they could achieve their single aim of destroying the enemy's entire army.

On the evening of 5 February, after covering 275 km in thirty-three hours, the 4th Armoured Brigade was astride the road, blocking the Italians' line of retreat south of Beda Fomm. The following morning, quite unsuspecting, the Italians walked into the trap and, as their columns appeared, they were shot down.

They had nearly four times as many Cruiser tanks as the British, but they were moving in batches and presented an easy target to the 4th Armoured Brigade. And while the British took full advantage of the rough country to protect themselves, the Italians kept closely to the road.

The battle raged all day and by the following morning sixty Italian tanks had been crippled, forty more abandoned and the last of Graziani's army was surrendering *en masse*. Rarely has the commander of such a mighty army suffered such a humiliating and total defeat. The British and Australians, only 3000 strong, had lost only three of their twenty-nine tanks and had captured another 20,000 Italians, 120 tanks and 216 guns. Benghazi was occupied on 6 February, and two days later El Agheila.

In two months, two British divisions had advanced 800 km and routed an army of ten divisions. They suffered about 2000 casualties, but captured 130,000 of the enemy, nearly 400 tanks and over 800 guns. The Royal Air Force, too, had played its part, keeping the skies clear of enemy planes and so allowing O'Connor's tanks and armoured cars to outflank the Italians unhindered. In the process, they destroyed some 150 enemy aircraft.

O'Connor had shown a similar flair and audacity to that which General Rommel would display in the months afterwards, earning him the same affection and respect for his fearless and inspiring direction of the battle from the very front.

There was now nothing within his own sphere of operations to stop Wavell from pushing on into Tripolitania and capturing Tripoli, the country's largest city and a most important target. But he was never allowed the chance.

General Metaxas had died on 29 January 1941 and his successor as Premier of Greece, Alexandros Korizis, had no similar qualms about accepting British military aid. When Churchill repeated his offer, he accepted it with alacrity. It meant, however, that the troops he needed would have to come from North Africa and this, in turn, meant calling a halt to the triumphant campaign which was also the only theatre in the world where British Commonwealth ground forces were actually in action against the enemy.

Wavell's new orders, issued by the War Cabinet in London immediately after the capture of Benghazi, were to concentrate his major effort on giving aid to Greece. And in spite of his limited resources, Churchill also directed that he should press on with the plans that already existed for occupying the islands of the Italian Dodecanese, as well as holding the frontier between Cyrenaica and Tripolitania which was now the western extremity of the Egyptian base.

Wavell already had under his command Australian troops. The 6th Australian Division had taken part in the rout of the Italians in the Western Desert and the 7th and 9th Australian Divisions (the 7th minus a brigade which was in England and a battalion which was still in Australia) were in Palestine. There was also a New Zealand Division in Egypt.

The armoured units, all from the British army, were a key component of any desert fighting force but those which Wavell had under his command were in a dismal state. Their engines were nearly burnt out and their tracks at the end of their lives. When new tracks were finally delivered, specially made in Australia, they were found to be the wrong size and were useless. There were no tank transporters so that the tanks had to make their own way into battle over far greater distances than were ever intended for them, over country that took months off their useful working lives, before they even came within range of the enemy. And the artillery of one of the Australian divisions had not yet even received any guns.

Wavell tried to make the best use he could of his slender resources. His armoured formation was split into two, with the better half going to Greece and the rest remaining in Cyrenaica; and his entire infantry, except for a single division, was allocated to the Greek expedition and the assault on the Dodecanese. This meant that, for the entire defence of the western frontier in North

Africa, he had allotted only one division of infantry and part of the 2nd Armoured Division. It was a risky decision, but he had little choice.

His rationalisation was along the lines that he had so small a force at his disposal that risks had to be taken somewhere and that the least dangerous place to take them was North Africa. He doubted whether the Germans would entrust their armoured units to the Italian Navy which was then running supplies to Tripoli. Even if they did, he was convinced that they would not be able to concentrate enough forces for a counter-offensive before May. This gave him two months to prepare his small force for its watchman role and then to keep a foot in the door while reinforcements were rushed in to fight off the attack.

There was certainly no doubt that the troops he was leaving in Cyrenaica would need every minute of that two months to prepare themselves. They shared one attribute above all others — they were the rawest, most ill-trained, ill-equipped men under his command.

The Armoured Brigade was equipped with worn-out light and medium tanks of their own, plus a few which had been captured from the Italians. Three of the Australian brigades were newly formed, and the whole hotch-potch force was commanded by a general, Sir Philip Neame, who knew little about desert fighting or armoured warfare.

Wavell was far from happy with the situation in Cyrenaica, and his first meeting with Neame did nothing to reassure him. Neame's dispositions of his force were downright absurd and Wavell was forced to order him to make substantial changes. Moreover, the tanks which the Armoured Division did have were either broken down or constantly breaking down. There was not a mobile striking force worth the name and nothing in reserve. Wavell returned to his headquarters deeply troubled and gave Neame instructions that his task would not even be to hold ground but just to keep his force intact, delay the enemy and inflict what casualties he could.

Neame had succeeded General Wilson who had been appointed commander of the expedition to Greece. His courage was never in doubt — he had won the Victoria Cross in World War I — but his ability as a senior commander has been severely questioned. He had not hidden his disappointment at being passed over for command of the Western Desert Force and he came to Cyrenaica from being

Commander-in-Chief, Palestine and Transjordan. His Headquarters were at Barce, north-east of Benghazi and some 25 km inland from the Mediterranean.

It had not been Wavell's intention that his Cyrenaican force should be quite so unskilled. His first order was that the battle-proven 6th Australian Division, which had taken part in the campaign against the Italians, should provide the western frontier defence force and that the 7th and 9th Australian Divisions would make up the contingent to go to Greece. But the Australian GOC in the Middle-East, General Sir Thomas Blamey, insisted that the Greek operation was so hazardous that his best division, the 6th, must be included in it. He had the right to overrule Wavell in this respect.

Wavell therefore had no choice but to relieve the 6th Division with one of the untried and half-equipped divisions. Even though he believed that the Germans would be unable to attack before May, he was still very troubled that when an attack did eventually and inevitably come, he would have to meet it without the 6th Division. About the only positive measures he could take were to reinforce his armoured units by the addition of another tank battalion equipped with Italian medium tanks captured in battle, and to begin rigorous training. No other reinforcements could be expected in the immediately foreseeable future.

Blamey wasted no time in putting under way a massive shake-down and reorganisation of the Australians under his command, all aimed at ensuring that only the best trained among them went to Greece. The main unit to receive his attention was the 9th Division, the most recently formed division in the AIF.

The decision to form this fourth division (in addition to the 6th, 7th and 8th) had been made in September, 1940 and many of its units had already been formed for either the 6th or 7th Divisions. It included the 18th Brigade (whose Headquarters and battalions had originally belonged to the 6th) and the 25th Brigade, which had been formed in England, mainly from unattached troops who had arrived in the same convoy as the 18th. The division was put under the command of Major-General H. D. Wynter who was already in England.

To complete the division, a third infantry brigade, as well as anti-tank, sapper, medical and supply and service units, was to be raised in Australia. The whole division was then to be assembled in the Middle East.

This last part of Cabinet's decision, however, was not at all to Blamey's liking. He was particularly critical of the idea of combining the two brigades in England, which included some of the best trained troops in the AIF, with units that had not even been raised yet, let alone trained. He insisted that the third division must come from units which had already been formed.

Instead of this newly formed brigade, the 24th Brigade, with an anti-tank regiment and other supporting units, was taken away from the 8th Division, which was then in Australian waiting to be sent to Singapore; and the still-to-be-formed units were allocated to the 9th in the Middle East. Wynter himself sailed from England for the Middle East on 16 November, taking the 18th Brigade.

His Divisional Headquarters were established at Julis in Palestine on Christmas Eve and the remainder of the division arrived in instalments from then until the second week in March when the 25th Brigade landed. By then it didn't even belong to the 9th Division.

It was this newly born 9th Division on which Blamey concentrated his attention when juggling the Australian forces to ensure that Wavell was left with the least effective and worst trained troops in Cyrenaica. And it was the 9th Division, reshaped and almost unrecognisable when it emerged from his surgery, that was to so distinguish itself in the coming months.

Of the original three brigades, only one still remained with the new 9th; and of the battalions that now made up its infantry, not one had originally been raised for the 9th. The 18th and 25th Brigades were transferred to the 7th, which was to go to Greece; and in return, the 20th and 26th Brigades went from the 7th to the 9th. The division's infantry now consisted of the 20th, 24th and 26th Brigades and its artillery of the 2/7th, 2/8th and 2/12th Field Regiments, and the 2/3rd Anti-Tank Regiment.

The immediate and tangible result of these military musical chairs was the overnight disappearance of what little *esprit de corps* already existed. Nobody in the new 9th Division had any illusions about why they were there — they were the troops least fitted to be sent out on a job that really mattered.

The 20th and 26th Brigades felt bitter resentment at being

plucked from a division of which they were very proud. Even the number of the new division rankled. Just as individual soldiers were proud if they had low numbers because it showed that they had been quick to enlist, so they took pride in belonging to a low numbered unit which was older and so had more battle experience and tradition. For the 20th and 26th Brigades, being taken away from the 7th and given to the unweaned 9th was like being punished and demoted.

In fact the 20th Brigade had been in Palestine for only three months after being formed in May 1940; and the 26th had been there for two months and had been formed in July 1940. The 24th had been formed for the same time as the 26th, but had been there for only three weeks. None of the units had been issued with its full complement of arms and most of its training had been carried out with toy guns — although they had at least fired live automatic weapons on the range. None of the battalions had been exercised as units and their officers were virtually untrained in battle management. They were not quite the troops that a commander would have chosen to challenge the strength of the Axis.

The morale of the division was far from helped by Blamey's unfortunate choice of words when he announced the formation of the new 9th Division. It was, he said, 'a temporary expedient only'. About the only thing that could be calculated to destroy pride in the unit still further was to tell its officers and men that the whole set-up was only make-shift anyway.

The 18th Brigade had originally belonged to the 6th Division which had fought so well in the Western Desert in Wavell's campaign. It had arrived there in mid-January, under its commander Brigadier Leslie Morshead, to join the Allied troops poised and waiting to capture the fort of Bardia where the Italians were safely bottled up.

It was the first brigade of General Wynter's division to arrive in the desert and before the other two arrived Wynter had been removed from command. He had been taken seriously ill and Blamey ordered his replacement.

Blamey's choice for the job was Major-General John Northcott, the Deputy Chief of the General Staff of the Australian army, but Northcott's chief, General Sturdee, refused to release him. Blamey's second choice then was a man who was not a professional soldier at all, but who, as World War I historian, Dr C. E. W. Bean, aptly described him, was a man 'in whom the traditions of the British Army had been bottled from his childhood like light-corked champagne.'

That choice was the commander of the 18th Brigade, Brigadier Leslie Morshead, who a few short months later was to make his name a household word throughout Australia.

Morshead was a good and obvious choice for the job. Wynter had been promoted over him to command the division, but he had served him loyally. He was an unashamedly strict disciplinarian, nicknamed Ming the Merciless by his unappreciative subordinates, and he believed that battles and campaigns are won by leadership and discipline and, above all, by sheer guts.

He was, and never ceased to be throughout the siege of Tobruk when he commanded the Fortress, unsparing, unforgiving, harsh in his criticism, yet quick to praise when he thought it due. He hated pretentiousness and humbug and gradually, as they each came to know one another better, he earned first the grudging respect and then the very real and strong affection of his men.

He might well have expected to be Blamey's first choice and probably would have been except that he was not a professional soldier. Like that other controversial Australian leader of World War II, General Gordon Bennett, he had lived and breathed things military all his adult life. A schoolteacher in his younger days, he had gone into business between the wars and had been the Sydney manager of the Orient Line. For seven years he had also commanded a militia brigade. When war broke out he was fifty, older than most of his fellow officers, but he was immediately appointed a Brigade Commander in the 6th Division. There were few generals who could match his experience in battle.

Physically he was not a big man and he looked almost mild at casual acquaintance. But when he looked at you, one of his subordinates recalls, it was like a lance piercing into you. The eyes were cold and ruthless and he could make even a mild dressing down feel like an hour with the Inquisition. He was quite disinterested in how history remembered him and years later preferred not to release any of his private diaries and papers from his days in the desert and at Tobruk.

In spite of all this Blamey, like many regular soldiers, believed that anyone who was not a professional soldier was somehow not a 'proper' soldier, that he could never be quite as skilful a commander, quite as clever a tactician, quite as galvanising a leader of men.

After the upheaval in the 9th Division, it was ordered to be ready to move to Cyrenaica immediately to relieve the 6th Division, which was to prepare to join the expedition to Greece. The only units of the 9th that were not to go to Libya at once were the field artillery, which were neither trained nor even equipped. First to move, on the very day after it was transferred to the 9th Division, was the 20th Brigade, commanded by Brigadier J. J. Murray. It had been in the Middle East for marginally longer than the other brigades and so was allotted the forward zone. The other two brigades were to take up garrison duties in Derna and Tobruk and were to be given intensive training to prepare them for battle.

Murray's Headquarters pulled out of their camp in the first road convoy at the start of the long journey ahead of them. That same evening the brigade's 2/13th Battalion left by train, rattling westwards towards the desert, over the Suez Canal, through Cairo and Alexandria, past a place called El Alamein that meant nothing at that time of the war, through depressing, fly-blown stops with names like Galal, Fuka and Bagush, and finally, in the cold and drizzle, reaching Mersa Matruh, the end of the desert line.

For most of the men arriving, the sight of the town was an eye-opening experience. The little port was scarred by bombing, many of its buildings empty shells, and the whole town was ringed with barbed wire and anti-tank ditches and protected by minefields.

Most of the brigade arrived in Mersa Matruh on 2 March and, after a brief and damp rest there, transferred to trucks on the following day. From early morning, four long convoys headed out at the start of a tiring 200 km journey along the coast road to Buq Buq, their first staging post. They rested there overnight and the next day crossed the frontier into Libya and drove straight through to Tobruk.

Tobruk was an even more desolate sight than Mersa Matruh. The ravages of the battle to secure it were everywhere and as though to remind the brigade that they were there to fight a desert war, a violent sandstorm blew up, blotting out the sun, penetrating every crevice in their clothes and bodies.

They had a day's rest at Tobruk and then, on 6 March, moved

out again, this time heading for Derna, Mussolini's 'Riviera of the South', a pretty little port of white houses, bougainvillea and flowering shrubs. Before they reached the town, however, they were suddenly and without warning attacked by five Heinkel aircraft which came in from over the sea and repeatedly bombed and strafed them for half an hour. Damage was mercifully light, but two men were killed and one wounded, a salutary warning, if one was needed, that the enemy was still very close.

The convoys moved on immediately after the Heinkels had departed and by early afternoon were descending the steep escarpment into Derna on the magnificent Via Balbia, the highway spanning Italian North Africa from Tunisia in the west right across to Egypt in the east. This time they did not delay but zig-zagged their way back up the escarpment to the west of the town where they made camp for the night.

Next day they moved on to Tocra, passing unexpectedly through green and fertile country, incongruous after the desert and tended by Italian settlers who worked on as if the war had never happened.

Finally, on 8 March, the Australians were drawing close to their destination. They entered the tree-lined outskirts of Benghazi, driving down an avenue of leafy eucalypts and then, almost as fast, on into the desert to the area around Agedabia. The 2/13th Battalion was sent to the coast near Beda Fomm, scene of the final humiliating defeat of the Italian North African army, less one company which was dropped off at Barce to guard Cyrenaica Command Headquarters.

Meanwhile, Divisional Headquarters had just arrived at Tobruk, twenty-four hours after Morshead and his Chief of Staff, Colonel C. E. M. Lloyd, had been briefed by Neame. The Australians were to take over responsibility immediately for all the fighting troops in western Cyrenaica from General Sir Iven Mackay of the 6th.

That was pleasing enough to Morshead, who was determined that his troops would have reached a sufficient state of readiness by the time the Germans advanced against them; but what drove him into a fury was Neame's rider that he was only to be responsible for the fighting troops for a short time. At the earliest possible opportunity, probably only ten days hence, the Headquarters of 2nd Armoured Division would replace him in command in the frontier area.

Worse still was that Neame told him that he was to move his

Headquarters to Gazala to supervise the training of his troops, but that 20th Brigade would remain in the forward area — outside his control. It would become the main infantry frontier force, yet it would not be under his, or indeed any Australian's, command. Morshead did not mince his words and told Neame bluntly that he was 'not impressed with this arrangement'.

But for all his anger, Morshead did not have the right, as Gordon Bennett had in Singapore, of direct access to the Australian Government. And his greater concern and most immediate task was to get on with the training of his men. It was very likely that, within a couple of months, they would be facing the enemy. At the same time, he had somehow to improve the level of equipment with which each man and unit had been issued.

He was ably helped by his senior officer, Lloyd, a big, bluff man, friendly and down-to-earth, who was the ultimate realist when it came to getting jobs done. A professional soldier for more than twenty years, he was the quintessential staff officer, protecting his general from the inessential, ensuring always that his wishes were carried out.

Brigadier Murray and his 20th Brigade arrived at the Headquarters of the 6th Division's 17th Brigade on 9 March and the relief had been completed before midnight that same day. Their new position was in sand dunes and rolling country near the small harbour of Mersa Brega, surrounded by swamp. So far, there were no visible flaws in Wavell's plan.

If intelligence reports spoke of a rapid build-up of an Axis force in Tripoli and, disturbingly, of a significant increase in the number of German armoured troops and vehicles, Wavell drew comfort from the fact that there was only one road along which the enemy could come and that shortage of water would present serious difficulties to any sizeable force moving east towards the Cyrenaican border.

Intelligence, in any case, was very incomplete. It had at first been left to the French, with their special knowledge of the region, but when France capitulated there was no one to replace them and worthwhile intelligence virtually ceased. Even aerial reconnaisance was impossible when the German Air Force controlled the skies over North Africa.

One subject on which intelligence was woefully lacking was

information about the young German general called Rommel who had been ordered to North Africa with two armoured divisions to try and stop the rot that had set into the Axis fortunes with the defeat of Marshal Rodolfo Graziani's army.

Wavell knew that he had arrived, knew that he was a relatively junior commander with a brief but brilliant record as a tactician, but attached no special importance to him. It was perhaps his most significant mistake in the North African campaign.

The Superb Tactician

General Franz Halder, the German Chief of Staff, described Rommel, without affection, as 'this soldier gone stark mad.' But if he caused the German High Command endless problems in other theatres by his refusal to turn away from a potential victory, no matter what his instructions, it did not belittle for one moment his brilliance as a commander in the desert.

On 3 February Hitler, incensed by the extent of the Italian defeat in North Africa, no longer waited for the formality of Mussolini's agreement. He gave orders that a division of infantry, with two battalions of medium and light tanks, was to be sent there at the earliest opportunity. What was more, a complete armoured division of Germans would be added to this force.

The Italians were told of this decision on 5 February and the following day, the day of the final ignominy for the Italians at Beda Fomm, Rommel was called to Hitler and told that he was to be prepared to take command of two mechanised divisions.

He was an inspired choice. Erwin Rommel was fifty and had been a professional soldier all his life. He was one of the officers selected to remain in the greatly diminished German army after Germany's defeat in World War I and he became an expert on infantry tactics. He taught at an infantry school and then at a War Academy, wrote a definitive manual on infantry tactics and — his specialty — the employment of highly mobile tactics as opposed to position warfare. As Hitler's power grew, Rommel became first an adviser to the Hitler Youth Organisation and, finally, the commander of Hitler's bodyguard.

Yet is spite of this exposure to the enormous personal power that could be enjoyed and abused by those close to the Fuehrer, he remained throughout his career a man of the highest principles. He fought, in his own words, *krieg ohne hass*, war without hatred, and it was this chivalry as much as his courage and insistence on leading from the front, which earned the ungrudging admiration of his men and his enemy alike, to an extraordinary degree in time of war.

It caused problems for the propagandists at times: it is not helpful to actually like the commander of one's enemy. But word very quickly travelled back down the lines that here was an honourable man who treated his captured and injured prisoners with courtesy and care. It manifested itself in such ways as the occasion, during the siege of Tobruk, when Australian soldiers actually crossed over the the enemy lines during a brief truce and helped the Germans to carry their own dead and wounded back to the ambulances and First Aid Posts.

Yet it was a brutal war and none fought it so hard as Rommel. He was not, in fact, Commander-in-Chief in North Africa, for Libya remained Italian territory. That position was still held by an Italian, Marshal Gariboldi, who had replaced the hapless Graziani. On paper at least, Rommel was allowed only to 'advise' the Italians and he was supposed to receive all his tactical instructions from Gariboldi; in reality he was his own master, frequently ignoring even orders from Berlin if he thought the situation warranted it.

He was a brave and clever commander with a flair for mounting attacks on his enemy's flanks. It was a talent that few on the Allied side of the battlefield were quick to grasp, but which would have been very clear after even a cursory reading of his manual. And he was willing to take risks and to seize and take advantage of opportunities that suddenly presented themselves — all quite alien characteristics for a senior German officer. At first, Allied Intelligence seemed quite unable to grasp this, just as they failed to realise that here was an adversary who was prepared to act quite independently of any higher authority.

Wavell had no difficulty assessing what the German High Command intended to do in the desert; he was quite wrong in his estimate of what Rommel might do.

Rommel received his orders from Hitler on 6 February and on 8 February the first German forces sailed from Italy. Rommel himself took two days' leave with his family and then left for

Tripoli, travelling by way of Rome where he conferred with the German Military Attaché and the Italians. It was in Rome that he announced that his first line of defence would be at Sirte, 250 km west of the nearest Allied positions at El Agheila.

He arrived in Tripoli on 12 February, forty-eight hours ahead of his first units. Hitler had been explicit in explaining that his primary purpose — indeed his only purpose — in sending German troops into North Africa was to prevent Wavell from overrunning the whole of Libya and conquering Tripolitania and Tripoli as well as Cyrenaica. Rommel was therefore to do nothing but carry out reconnaisance and be prepared to resist an assault on Tripolitania by Wavell's forces.

In selecting Rommel for the task Hitler must have known that to follow such orders was wholly alien to his general's character. Rommel arrived in Tripoli and saw immediately that Wavell's force was grossly overstretched. He reasoned, correctly, that the explanation for the sudden Allied halt at the Cyrenaican border was that its forces had been depleted still further, probably because of the demands of the Greek campaign.

He was certain that if he struck quietly he would catch the Allies off balance and, by carrying out his unique brand of 'lightning warfare', could put them to flight. Their commander, General Neame, Rommel knew to be a man quite inexperienced in desert warfare; and Intelligence reports suggested that he was hidebound and dated in his tactical approach. Rommel therefore planned his attack for the end of March and immediately set about training his men in the art of mobile desert warfare.

There were many logistic problems and Rommel was soon made aware — though he never really learned the lesson — that the greatest obstacle to a successful campaign in the desert was not the harsh environment or the total lack of cover, or even the strength of the enemy, but the difficulty of maintaining supplies.

There were unexpected difficulties, like those associated with operating machinery and transport in the desert. Vehicles arrived with twin tyres on the rear wheels and the razor-sharp desert stones got trapped between them and tore them to shreds. Diesel engines, far preferable to petrol in the desert because of the problems of vaporisation, dust and heat, were not fitted to any of the first vehicles to be delivered to North Africa — because it was feared that they would overheat! And the first tanks did not even have oil filters.

They were the problems that could be fairly quickly resolved, as could the health problems that arose because the troops were not being given enough fresh food. Throughout the campaign the Germans had difficulty keeping fruit fresh. It arrived at the front rotten and inedible and there were never enough lemons, vital to the men's diet, to satisfy each person.

On 19 February, Rommel's force became officially known as the Africa Corps. Newly arrived troops were ordered out of Tripoli as soon as they landed and were sent forward to Sirte, his chosen first line of defence. He wanted the British to know that they were now facing Germans in the field, who were very different opponents from the capitulating Italians.

The planned Russian campaign had siphoned off a considerable part of the armoured formation that Rommel might otherwise have expected, but it was still much stronger than the depleted 2nd Armoured Division which was all that Wavell could put up against him. Among its most deadly weapons were eight-wheeled armoured cars operated by the reconnaisance units which proved to be more than a match for the six-wheeled cars of the Allies, both in hitting power and cross-country performance.

There was only one area in which the Allied force had supremacy over the Germans and Italians and that was the artillery, whose performance during the coming months was often nothing less than superb.

In the air, the Allies were so outnumbered as to make their puny force seem almost irrelevant. A sizeable air force of Stuka divebombers and Messerschmitt fighters was on its way to aid Rommel, in addition to the long-range bombers that he could call on from Sicilian-based fields. As soon as the reinforcements arrived, they were ordered to move forward to bases closer to the Cyrenaican frontier from where they could harass the enemy. An early target were Allied petrol tankers moving cumbersomely along the coast road. Rommel was as conscious of the need to deny fuel to his enemy as he was to secure sufficient for himself.

Whether Churchill would have withdrawn his generous offer of aid to the Greeks had he known of the German plan to reinforce the Italians with a crack armoured force can be nothing more than conjecture. But what is indisputable is that he did nothing to change his plans when the new danger that confronted his troops became apparent.

More significant, from Australia's point of view, was that neither he nor anyone else in London or the Middle East — and that included the Australian Commander-in-Chief himself — advised the Australian Government that one of its units was suddenly at grave risk. Blamey, just as much as his British counterparts, seemed to be obsessed with the Greek campaign to the exclusion of everything else.

Meanwhile, back in the desert, Morshead wasted no time before acquainting himself with the units that he had inherited from General Mackay and the territory that he was charged with defending. What he saw filled him with apprehension.

While his reconnaisance aircraft and intelligence reports, scanty as they were, reported a constant build-up of armoured fighting vehicles (AFVs) near the Tripolitanian border and a steady movement of shipping into Tripoli as well as the small ports east of Tripoli, he was himself coming increasingly under attack from the dive-bombing and high-level bombing raids which grew fiercer by the day.

The German aircraft were aggressive and clearly well briefed and he was compelled to move his Headquarters under pressure from their bombs. British armoured cars were also heavily bombed and when engineers went out through the perimeter to repair them they came under withering fire from machine guns firing along fixed lines.

Far from supporting Wavell's contention that the enemy could not possibly launch any serious attack before May, all the evidence that confronted him suggested a massive build-up in preparation for a major offensive. More than 200 tanks had arrived in Tripoli and a hastily modified appreciation of the situation by Middle East Headquarters warned that El Agheila was likely to be an early target — perhaps even before the end of March — from which more ambitious operations could be launched.

Morshead's force, by comparison 'completely without hitting power', as his Chief Staff Officer put it, didn't even have the strength to mount an aggressive reconnaissance patrol, let alone put up a serious defence against the kind of force being marshalled by the Germans.

Spare parts for AFVs and conventional transport were in chronically short supply, and when Morshead sent two trucks off to Tobruk with a shopping list of spares, they returned several days later bearing nothing but a speedometer cable. Benghazi had already had to be abandoned as a supply port because of constant enemy bombing, leaving only Tobruk, more than 650 km from the front line. The coast road between Benghazi and Agedabia came to be so heavily strafed that the Australians christened it 'bomb alley'. The strain was beginning to tell.

Italian equipment, abandoned by the fleeing troops of Marshal Graziani only weeks earlier, was commandeered and put to use. One battalion, which had never been issued with a telephone or cable, had 32 km of wire and sixteen sets of telephones working — all Italian. Other equipment pilfered included dozens of motor cycles, weapons, ammunition, camouflage sheets and tools.

All through the campaign, however, there were accidents occurring from these Italian weapons and ammunition in spite of dire warnings from Headquarters. Many soldiers sustained serious eye injuries when they fired rifles they had picked up on the battlefield where they had been discarded by the Italians.

Amongst the Italian equipment were some 1877 rifles the bolts of which, when they were closed, left the wall of the cartridge exposed. If the rifle was even slightly dirty after lying in the sand and especially if the barrel was choked with sand, the risk of the cartridge exploding in the firer's eye was great.

An assortment of guns, from anti-tank weapons to big field guns was pressed into use and was quickly dubbed 'the bush artillery'. They played an important part in the defence of Tobruk after the siege began, but they were fearsome weapons.

They came in an assortment of sizes and their reliability was closely related to their age and the time they had lain in the sand. They were frequently so corroded by the desert weather that they were useless and very dangerous, but many were made serviceable by the workshops. A school run by a British unit, the Nottinghamshire Sherwood Rangers, gave instruction in the handling of this 'bush artillery' which was fired not by the gunners but by the Australian infantry.

General Neame gave instructions that discarded Italian weapons of any size were to be left well alone, but fortunately the Australians, in particular, ignored his orders and continued to carry or drag them back. The purpose of the lessons was to teach men how to load and fire these weapons 'with the least risk to the firer and the maximum to the enemy.' Prematurely detonating ammunition for the anti-tank and field guns caused many injuries before it was laid down that the only safe was to fire them was to fix 30 m of rope to the trigger and retire behind a sandbag wall or take cover in a ditch or trench. With time and practice, the Allied troops became remarkably proficient with their secondhand weaponry.

Disobeying Neame's instructions about bringing back the Italian weapons was the least of the activities of the Australians which earned them the disapproval of the overwhelmingly British staff of Neame's Headquarters. Neame himself made it clear that whatever he thought of them as soldiers, he was not enamoured with them as people.

There was hardly a campaign where Australians fought during World War II where criticism was not levelled against them for their behaviour. The charges ranged from looting and drunkenness to theft, rape and, in New Guinea, even sacrilege. In North Africa if was looting, drunkenness, shooting in the streets and even shooting at servants in a British officers' mess.

By the end of March Neame, who had never showed much sympathy for the Australians, was so incensed by the reports he was receiving of Australian behaviour towards the civilians they encountered as they travelled westwards from Egypt to the front, that he wrote a personal letter to General Morshead. It was a long-standing grievance that went back to the first days of the Australian presence in Cyrenaica when they had taken part in the capture of the little port of Derna. They were accused there of committing a long list of very serious civil offences that included wholesale looting.

The fact that the unfortunate inhabitants of Derna had already been looted on three separate occasions since the war began paled into insignificance compared with the reports of what the Australians had done.

Now Neame wrote that parties of Australians had entered Benghazi and cases of drunkenness had occurred again there. It wasn't simply that the Australians, who were the first to admit that they liked a drink, got noisy when they were drunk.

'Since the 20th Infantry Brigade of the 9th Australian Division was moved to the area,' Neame wrote indignantly, 'numerous disgraceful incidents have occurred in Barce.' (Barce was the location of Neame's Headquarters and men of the 20th had been deployed there as a guard.) 'Drunkenness, resisting military police, shooting in the streets, breaking into officers' messes and threatening and shooting at officers' mess servants — even a drunken soldier has come into my own Headquarters and disturbed my staff.

'This state of affairs reached a climax yesterday when the streets were hardly safe or fit to move in. I consider it disgraceful that I and my staff should have our attention and time absorbed by these disciplinary questions at a time when we have to consider fighting the Germans and Italians.'

Neame concluded, 'I am at a loss for words to express my contempt for those who call themselves soldiers who behave thus... and their officers are equally to blame, as they show themselves incapable of commanding their men if they cannot enforce these things, discipline, obedience of orders and soberness. I must tell you now that the CIGS (Chief of the Imperial General Staff, General Dill) and C-in-C (Wavell), when visiting me here, were accosted in the street by a drunken Australian soldier. I myself have had the same experience in Barce.

'Your Division will never be a useful instrument of war unless and until you can enforce discipline... and all the preparations of the Higher Command may be rendered useless by the acts of an undisciplined mob behind the front.'

If Morshead thought, as he wrote in his diary, that Neame was coming on a little strong for what the Australians had apparently done, he equally thought that the Australians were in need of more discipline. He placed all towns, villages and native camps out of bounds to Australian troops and ordered his senior officers to restore discipline by 'firmness and adequate punishment'.

One of his difficulties was that it had been clearly established that the disciplining of Australian soldiers was a matter exclusively for the Australian administration to deal with. Ultimate responsibility lay with the Australian Commander-in-Chief, not the British commander of the area. The only practical way of controlling soldiers in towns when they were not formed up was with the aid of military police, but Morshead had none. The division's Provost Corps was at Tobruk and there was no transport to bring it forward.

In his diary, rather irrelevantly, Morshead wrote that he couldn't help feeling that it was the same old story of giving a dog a bad name... like the case of the Australian private who entered the officers' mess at Barce. He had been accompanied by two British privates, but Neame had made no mention of them.

To Neame, Morshead complained face to face about his blatantly anti-Australian attitude which, he said, had permeated his entire staff. He told him that he intended to forward his letter to Blamey, possibly even to the government in Australia and to Wavell. It was a strong stand, but it didn't refute a single one of the complaints which Neame had outlined.

Rommel, meanwhile, had paid a flying visit to Berlin on 19 March and had seen Hitler. He asked for reinforcements so that he could occupy the whole of Cyrenaica, which he felt was within his grasp, but he was told that he could expect nothing more than the armoured division which was already on its way to North Africa. In very unambiguous terms he was also told again to bide his time and to wait and see what the British and Australians would do. His role was still essentially a defensive one with the possible addition of a drive down the highway to capture Benghazi at some date to be fixed.

Instead, he returned to Libya more determined than ever to go on the offensive immediately and he ordered preparations for an attack on El Agheila. Until then there had been only a few direct confrontations with a small number of casualties on both sides, and for several days there had been no contact with the enemy at all. There had been frequent *khamsins*, the choking, blinding sandstorms that swept out of the Sahara, bringing visibility down to arm's length and both armies to a frustrating standstill. Throughout the long campaign, neither army managed to improvise a reliable way of making use of the *khamsins* for cover.

On 20 March Wavell correctly read his opponent's intentions and reported to the Chiefs of Staff that an attack on the frontier seemed imminent and that if his advanced troops were driven from their present positions, there would be no point in holding positions south of Benghazi.

To prevent a pocket of the enemy looking over his shoulder, Wavell ordered an attack on the oasis of Giarabub, 300 km south of Tobruk, which was still held by the Italians. They had been causing no trouble and would probably have sat out the campaign contentedly unless the Germans galvanised them into action.

The garrison surrendered after a token resistance and this was to be the last offensive action that the Allies would take in the desert for some time.

At the same time Wavell ordered his tanks forward to the front, but with no transporters they had to travel under their own power and they began to break down in alarming numbers. Most of them were in such a condition that it was not even worth the engineers putting in new engines. Gear boxes and transmissions, in particular, were worn to the point where they scarcely functioned, even in the tanks that were still operational.

The armoured cars, the six-wheel Marmon-Harringtons, fared equally badly on the long hike to the front. Their 30 hp Ford V-8 motors proved reliable, but their suspension couldn't cope with the sustained desert conditions. When they eventually came up against the German eight-wheelers they failed in almost every respect to match their efficiency, reliability and fire-power. The German cars were much faster and more efficient in the desert as well as being more heavily armed and armoured.

In the air, Cyrenaica Command had just 30 aeroplanes, including a squadron of Hurricanes at Bu Amud which was intended for the defence of Tobruk. The only airfield anywhere near the troops at the front was at Agedabia, between Benghazi and El Agheila, but it couldn't be used at night. It took the Germans a very short time to discover this and every morning at first light and every evening at dusk, they came over and bombed and strafed it. Without even taking account of the Italian Air Force, the Germans had ninety Messerschmitt fighters, including the very latest aircraft, and more than eighty bombers in North Africa with the back-up available on Sicily.

In fact the Royal Air Force, realising the hopelessness of their situation, moved back from the front on 22 March to prevent being swamped and losing all their aircraft when the German push began.

The battlefield on which the North African war was fought was a 1000-km long strip of land bordered on the north by the

Mediterranean and on the south by the desolate and almost impassable mass of the desert and the Sahara. Only a few oases deep in the desert took either side away from this narrow strip and every battle of significance was fought within 80 km of the sea and most of them much closer. Approximately halfway along the battlefield, at the eastern end of Libya, was the city of Tobruk.

Much of the country over which the desert war was fought was extremely difficult and dangerous to move across, let alone fight in. From the Egyptian frontier with Libya, the single road worthy of the name zig-zagged tortuously up the 152-metre escarpment to a plateau which stretched, with occasional breaks, from Bardia in the east to Gazala.

Immense sand dunes and escarpments, often so steep that they were quite inaccessible to any form of motorised transport; *wadis*, those dried-up rivers that had cut swathes sometimes hundreds of metres into the rock; towering cliff faces with sheer drops far into the valley below; all combined to make the coastal strip a hellish place to fight. And, from the escarpment southwards, seeming to stretch endlessly, lay the desert.

Historically, the term Western Desert meant only the desert in the west of Egypt, but in the desert campaign it stretched from El Alamein in the east to Gazala far to the west.

The highway hugged the coast over most of its distance and much of it was a brilliant feat of engineering by Italian engineers. It linked Egypt with Tunisia, 2500 km to the west, and maintained the link between the various countries and regions in that part of the Italian Empire.

At the western end of the plateau, near Gazala, the north and south escarpments gradually converged towards the northern side. Beyond Gazala, the terrain changed again. In the hump of Cyrenaica, stretching from Tmimi on the Gulf of Bomba to Benghazi and Ghemines on the western side, was the Green Mountain, or Jebel Achdar. Its slopes watered by the winter rain, the mountain had three sides, or escarpments, which were almost inaccessible, and a fourth side on the south which was rough and gouged out with gorges and valleys.

Going west yet again, along the shores of the Gulf of Sirte, were huge sand dunes and a chain of salt lakes and boggy marshes near the coast which turned into the most desolate land imaginable within a few kilometres of the sea. These extended from Agedabia to El Agheila, the frontier between the two Libyan provinces.

The high country in Cyrenaica was a boon to any defenders using it, but the Green Mountain area was also extremely vulnerable in turn to any enemy attempting to cut off its supply line. The only two ports on the hump were Derna, which was tiny, and Apollonia, which was even smaller, so everything had to come in by road from the east. To keep their positions opened, therefore, defenders would have had to come down on to the desert and fight from there.

At El Agheila itself there was a defile which was the only place between Cyrenaica and Tripoli where troops would be restricted. To bypass it meant a long and difficult march far enough from the mountain to be out of range of the defenders, and as El Agheila was the only entrance to Cyrenaica from the west along a road, it was clearly a key area to attack and defend.

When it was believed that the Italian armour was the most serious threat that could be expected, the defence of this area was thought to be simple enough. The western escarpment of the Green Mountain followed the coast down from Benghazi to Antelat where it gradually merged with rolling desert ideally suited for a tank battle which the Allies could expect to win. This was therefore the area where General Iven Mackay, commanding the frontier force, developed his defensive positions.

Even when Intelligence confirmed that it would not be an Italian force alone that had to be encountered, but a far superior German armoured contingent, possibly even a complete armoured brigade with more than 200 tanks, this instruction was not changed. It was not until General Morshead replaced Mackay, and realised at once that against this new threat his own force was pitifully small and hopelessly equipped, that the defence line was advanced to Marsa Brega, a small harbour to the north-east of El Agheila. So it was, as one historian put it, that 'when the enemy came through the front gate of Cyrenaica, the frontier watchdog was chained at Marsa Brega, twenty-five miles north-east of El Agheila.'

On 26 and 27 March the *khamsin* blew without respite. A sure tactical instinct told Rommel that the time to attack was very close. Fifth columnists among the Arabs who, for political reasons, had not been removed (for some months even some of the Italian settlers remained free), kept him fully informed of every movement behind the Allied lines, as well as continually sabotaging and stealing signal wires and any other unguarded equipment they came across.

Wavell viewed these Arabs with the greatest suspicion although his early briefings had suggested that in Cyrenaica at least he could count on their support against the Italians. There were very significant differences between the people of the two provinces which, it was said, would determine their allegiances. In Tripolitania, the population was largely engaged in the commercial farming of olives and other fruit and it was cosmopolitan enough to have come to terms, however uneasily, with the Italian colonial regime that had been forced upon it.

But in Cyrenaica it was very different. There the population was made up almost entirely of nomadic and semi-nomadic Arabs with a very deep resentment of any attempt to colonise them. As a consequence, the Italians had been forced to endure constant fighting and disruption, and it was from this that Intelligence rashly assumed that the Allies would be welcomed as saviours by the Arabs.

In fact, the Arabs viewed the British with even more suspicion than they did the Italians; and when they found that the Italians and then the Germans were willing to pay them for their loyalty, they became a very threatening fifth column behind the Allied lines. Eventually Wavell did allow them to be removed from sensitive areas, but not before they had performed an invaluable service to the Axis.

On 24 March Rommel struck and entered El Agheila, finding it empty of the enemy. The German High Command had told him to wait until reinforcements arrived and particularly until it was seen what developed in Greece and Crete, but he was too impatient. Using dummy tanks to make his armoured strength seem greater than it was (General Neame was doing the same), he launched his attack. The value of El Agheila to him, apart from giving him a toehold in Cyrenaica and a forward base for the next stage of the offensive, was that it had an ample water supply that he badly needed.

He met no serious opposition apart from a few pinpricks. A patrol from a British armoured unit approached El Agheila early in the morning without realising that the Germans were in the town, but when it was suddenly challenged, it fired a few rounds, killed a couple of the enemy, and withdrew at top speed in a hail of bullets.

Minutes later, a troop of armoured cars which were supporting the patrol, spotted enemy tanks approaching from the south. They hurriedly hid behind a mound and readied their anti-tank gun for action. They were barely in position when a German armoured car came straight over the top of the rise and opened fire on them. They retaliated at once, putting the German car out of action, but the Australian gunner behind the anti-tank gun was killed.

The patrol then hurriedly retreated to the safety of its own lines and plans for priming the minefield along the 14-km front that the Australians and the British cavalry were defending, were put into effect.

For a few days neither side made contact. The *khamsin* blew wildly, making any movement impossible, and it was not until 29 March that they clashed again. A reconnaisance troop of British six-wheel cars ran into two German eight-wheel cars, which immediately chased them. In the running battle that followed, the Germans put one of the six-wheelers out of action before withdrawing.

These exciting running battles, usually fought at 60 or 70 km/h in a cloud of dirt and sand, were to be a feature of the desert war for as long as it lasted. Their ingredients were speed, skilful driving, accurate shooting and always the element of surprise, with one or other side laying an ambush behind a mound or a sand dune that sent the survivors scurrying at top speed to another part of the desert.

As soon as Churchill heard of the occupation of El Agheila he despatched a cable to Wavell which showed only how ignorant London seemed to be of the real strength of the German force that was now threatening Cyrenaica. 'It is their habit to push on whenever they are not resisted,' Churchill wrote of the Axis forces. 'I presume you are only waiting for the tortoise to stick his head out far enough before chopping it off. It seems extremely important to give them an early taste of our quality.' That, at least, they were certainly about to do, but not at all in the way that Churchill had in mind.

Wavell was seriously hindered by poor intelligence reports. He did not have control of the skies which would have allowed him to make detailed aerial reconnaisance and reconnaisance from the ground in the desert was all but impossible.

On 31 March Rommel struck again. Neame had already issued orders for a hurried withdrawal should the need arise. (Only enemies retreat: one's own troops make controlled withdrawals.) Preparations were made for oiling or blowing up the wells and for the demolition of any supplies and installations that could not be taken with them. Australian and British engineers worked together at top speed to complete this work.

There was very good reason to be taking these precautions seriously for Morshead was 150 km away from the nearest Allied armoured division at a time when there was widespread agreement that whoever had the strongest armour was bound to win any battle in this part of the desert. In spite of all his pleas he had practically no armour, even to carry out reconnaisance, let alone take on a German panzer unit.

He was no better off with his signals equipment. Indeed he had so little of it that he was forced to use the Benghazi telephone exchange which was operated by Arab civilians. And his basic transport was so inadequate that three of his eight battalions could not even be moved. The 24th Brigade, which Morshead would have brought up to the front, was stuck in Tobruk.

Rommel watched the activity at Marsa Brega with considerable misgivings. It was naturally quite a strong defensive position to start with, and if the Allies could wire it and mine it sufficiently, it could become a very expensive proposition to take it. He still viewed his enemy with great respect for even though the extraordinary Allied successes had been scored over Italians whom he viewed with contempt, they had still won a stunning victory. At that stage he did not suspect just how vulnerable Neame's forces were, although he knew that Neame himself knew nothing of desert warfare.

Neame was given orders that he was not to hold ground if the threat to his force seemed too great and he obeyed this instruction to the letter. From the beginning of April, the British and Australians set off on an ignominious retreat in the direction of the Egyptian border. It became contemptuously known as the

Benghazi Handicap, as descriptive and accurate a name as the Adelaide River Stakes the following year when Australian troops ran away from the threat of a Japanese invasion at Darwin.

Wavell had written in his orders to Neame, 'The safe-guarding of your forces from a serious reverse and the infliction of losses and ultimate defeat of the enemy, are of much greater importance than the retention of ground. The re-occupation of Benghazi by the enemy, though it would have considerable propaganda and prestige value, would be of little military importance and it is certainly not worthwhile risking defeat to retain it'.

When the confrontation came the 2nd Armoured Division, the only armoured force that the Allies could put up against the might of Rommel's tanks, was so outnumbered and so harried by enemy aircraft that it was doomed from the start. Then it ran out of petrol. It contributed almost nothing to the battle and lost practically all its armour to boot.

It was at about quarter to eight on the morning of 31 March, a Monday morning, that an Australian outpost on Cemetery Hill outside Marsa Brega spotted the first approaching Germans, about 5000 m to the south-west. There appeared to be five tanks and two trucks, but pilots of scouting aircraft, keeping at a safe distance, reported at least 200 tanks and armoured cars, with swastika markings, heading towards Marsa Brega about 12 km away.

By nine o'clock the enemy could be clearly seen taking up positions around the town and the infantry patrols still outside the lines hurried back inside. By half-past ten the enemy infantry was closing in on Cemetery Hill and the first artillery fire was brought down on them.

The battle that followed was fierce and one-sided, its outcome never in doubt. At six that evening the full force of the German assault came, accompanied by dive-bombing attacks in which the defence shot down two of the attacking aircraft. At seven, enemy tanks and armoured cars entered Marsa Brega and the final defenders hurriedly withdrew to a distance about 14 km away. The Germans did not pursue them.

Not all the Allies in that part of the desert even knew that the Africa Corps had arrived in Libya, let alone that the offensive had begun. A long-range patrol near Msus saw trucks in the distance and assumed that they were either Free French or British. They turned to go and meet them, but sensed something seemed different. Both patrols then slowed down, as though sniffing the air to establish each other's identity, and in that moment both realised that the other was the enemy.

The Allied patrol, which came from the 3rd Indian Motor Brigade on the other side of the hump near Tobruk, was the first to move. They could see only too clearly that they were outnumbered and that the enemy were pulling a very dangerous field gun, so they wisely turned and ran, hotly pursued by the Germans.

An exciting chase followed, with both patrols moving at high speed, firing wildly, racing round the dunes until darkness came to the rescue of the Indians. The only casualty appeared to be a German truck which overturned.

That same day, Benghazi was evacuated and Churchill was predictably furious. In a message to Wavell he called the withdrawal 'most melancholy' and still showing no sign of comprehension of the true strength of Rommel's force — 'this blob which has come forward against you' — said caustically, 'I cannot understand how the enemy can have developed any considerable force at the end of this long, waterless coast road.'

As the retreat continued Churchill, with more reason, cabled his Secretary of State for Foreign Affairs, Anthony Eden, who was then in Athens, 'Far more important than the loss of ground (in North Africa) is the idea that we cannot face the Germans and that their appearance is enough to drive us back many scores of miles. this may react most evilly throughout the Balkans and Turkey... Sooner or later we shall have to fight the Huns. By all means make the best plan of manoeuvre, but anyhow fight.'

Rommel, meanwhile, had exactly the reverse problem. All he wanted to do was fight, while his superiors insisted on him doing nothing. The Italian Commander-in-Chief in particular, Marshal Gariboldi, was adamant that Rommel was to do nothing without his personal authority — until the German general called his bluff.

Gariboldi and Rommel were in conference, with the Italian as usual reiterating that Rommel was not fighting a private war and that he would do what he was told. In the middle of the meeting, a message was brought in to Rommel advising him that Keitel, the Supreme Commander of the Axis armies, had personally instructed that offensive action was to halt and that Gariboldi was to agree to this.

Rommel had no doubt that Gariboldi would agree immediately; indeed, he had been saying precisely this since the conference began. Instead the German looked across the table and announced that the High Command had promised him complete freedom of action. There was nothing more that Gariboldi could say.

Churchill's acid messages to Wavell and his exhortations to Eden were so many empty words when the Allies had no means of retaliating. Tanks cannot be fought with bare hands, nor run without tracks and petrol. There were basic flaws, as well, in the British chain of command which were not shared by the Germans. In particular they suffered from a command system which was painfully slow in making up its mind and worse, even slower in giving orders when its mind was made up. This was even more dangerous when Intelligence was poor, as it was then in North Africa, and when quick decisions were vital.

The German organisation, on the other hand, was admirably suited to desert warfare, for it laid great emphasis on a command system that could be varied almost from minute to minute. For a commander like Rommel who was always at the front studying the changing situation, it meant great flexibility.

Rommel revolutionised desert warfare. '*Blitzkrieg* came to the desert,' one writer said without exaggeration and certainly the Allies were learning fast that the methods they had used effectively against the Italians were not going to be good enough against the Germans.

Rommel, commanding in person as usual, sometimes from an armoured car, sometimes from a reconnaisance aircraft, pushed his little army up the coast road and across the desert, driving them at great speed and in widely dispersed small groups which he could bring together whenever a larger force was needed. The whole effect was of a superbly orchestrated production.

In a brilliant flanking movement on 7 and 8 April, Rommel captured Mechili and with it 3000 prisoners, including more than 100 Australians. Captured, too, was Major-General Gambier-Parry, the Mechili garrison commander, and even more seriously, for he was an outstanding soldier, General O'Connor, who had been the driving force behind the defeat of the Italians. Perhaps most humiliating of all, though, was the capture of a third general, Neame, the senior officer in Cyrenaica. As well as these prisoners, the Germans also acquired a large number of armoured vehicles, stores and ammunition.

The Italians were left to garrison Mechili and Rommel set out at once to run down the retreating Allies who were heading for the strongly fortified fortress of Tobruk. In an Order of the Day to his troops, he said, 'I am convinced that the enemy is giving way before us. We must pursue him with all our forces.'

His enemy was already withdrawing. When his advance troops came barking at the fence of Tobruk, they were greeted with a most hostile reception. Here at last he encountered the defiance that he had expected since he came over the frontier into El Agheila.

Retreat and Defence

Within nine days of taking Marsa Brega, Rommel had control of the whole of Cyrenaica except Tobruk. Within nine days, the resounding victories scored over the Italians had been wiped out and a victorious army had been reduced to a crowd of soldiers, deprived of three of their most senior generals, scurrying to get out of the way of the advancing Germans.

The reason was clear enough. The Allies had been emasculated by the removal of men, armour and materials for the Greek Campaign; and the Germans and Italians had an overwhelmingly superior force of armour, supremacy in the air and a brilliant commander. But in hindsight one wonders how much the attitude of the Allies themselves played its part. The odds against Tobruk holding out in the months that followed were just as slim, yet the fortress was held.

Rommel was experiencing disciplinary problems, most of them directly related to the seemingly impossible task of persuading the Italians to behave like soldiers and to face the enemy and fight instead of turning tail. The one unit of the Italian army in North Africa which fought with great bravery and distinction throughout the campaign was the artillery and Rommel was unstinting in his praise of them. The rest were hopeless.

For the present, however, when Mechili had been taken and the three generals were on their way back from the front for interrogation, Rommel had other things on his mind. He himself left Mechili very early in the morning on 10 April and drove straight to the Tobruk front.

'It was of great importance,' he wrote afterwards, 'to appear in strength before Tobruk and get our attack started as soon as possible for we wanted our blow to fall before the enemy had recovered his morale after our advance through Cyrenaica and before he could organise his defence of Tobruk.'

He ordered Tobruk to be encircled and then bombarded by the artillery to keep the Allies' heads down until he could mount the attack that he planned from the south-east. In fact some of his forces moved so fast that they arrived at Tobruk on the morning of the 10th to find that instead of the demoralised, beaten army they had expected, they were violently attacked by the defenders inside the Tobruk perimeter.

They had no knowledge of the defences and field works left by the Italians, which the Australians and British were now using and it was not until four days later that Rommel was able to obtain a map of them.

Although it didn't appear that way to the fleeing Allies, the Germans and Italians had not had it all their own way. The Panzer, or armoured, divisions were plagued with tanks breaking down and many of them had to be abandoned. If their crews were not quickly picked up, in the heat of the day, they had a water problem because individuals in the Panzer tanks carried no water bottles. Rather, each tank had a water container that held 5 litres per man.

As they moved towards Tobruk, they were constantly attacked by the Royal Air Force which, even though it had no supremacy in the air, fought bravely and untiringly for as long as it had the aircraft and somewhere to land them and take off. 'Their aeroplanes get on our nerves,' a lieutenant in a German Tank Regiment wrote in his diary. 'Ten or more attacks a day and we have no anti-aircraft, no fighters.' They were luxuries which Rommel had knowingly foregone when he decided to disobey Berlin and move against Wavell with only the men and resources that he had in his possession.

The captured diary of an *Oberst-Leutnant* in one of the German motorised divisions tells graphically the gruelling conditions that they endured as they pursued the Australians and British back to Tobruk.

'Sandstorm. Pitch black night. Sentry at fuel dump lost.' And the next day, 'Worse sandstorm. Everything covered in sand. Tents collapse.'

As his unit passed through an Arab village, what he described as a 'shilling shocker' occurred at the home of the Mufti, or Muslim priest. An Arab fired at the Mufti and his guests and was promptly shot dead by a German sentry.

After the fall of Marsa Brega the *Oberst-Leutnant* went off to inspect a minefield, took the wrong turn and found himself right in the middle of it. He managed to extricate himself and then began a strenuous march through the desert. 'Incredible track,' he wrote. 'Everything is stuck. In the darkness our tanks run over nine of our motor-cyclists. We lose our way.'

At 2 a.m., in pitch darkness, they halted to rest when they realised they were nowhere near a track. At dawn they set out to try and find it. 'Very hot. Repeated falling out of vehicles, lost in the lonesome desert. Fuel runs short. 5th Tank Regiment gets stuck.'

And next day, 'Detestable march on mine-infested track. Lt Hecker and pioneers hit mines. Casualties. At 0430 Rommel bellows and chases us forward, out of touch with the battalion across the stony desert. Only ten vehicles with us.'

When they finally reached Tobruk a heavy sandstorm was coming up and they tried to dig in in the rocky soil. The night was bitterly cold. Next morning a bridge was blown up by the Allies just as they reached it and again they were forced to take cover under blazing fire from the defenders inside the perimeter. One of the Germans' most senior generals in North Africa, Heinrich von Prittwitz, commander of the formidable 15th Armoured Division, was killed.

'Disastrous terrain,' the diary records. 'No cover whatsoever. Sandstorm. Heavy increase in casualties. As our tanks move up, they are already attacked by British bombers. Our own tanks nearly run over us. In addition to this, we receive the whole weight of British fire. Disgusting position. Digging in under heavy fire 200 m from enemy positions. Fierce British raids. Situation deteriorates.'

Twenty-four hours later he was killed.

For days Allied troops who had escaped ahead of the Germans and lost contact with their units, made their way into Tobruk, running the gauntlet of their own fire quite as much as that of the Germans. Some of these people had extraordinary escapes, constantly running into the enemy, taking cover in deep *wadis* by day and trying to move by compass alone under cover of darkness. It was precarious because there was no way of knowing, if the night was moonless, when they might walk over the vertical side of a deep *wadi*.

Some escaped in trucks and, when the going was good, they sped across the hard sand but then, without warning, they would be on sharp rocks, or worse, up to their axles in sand that suddenly turned soft and brought them to a bone-shattering halt. Many were captured or killed, but most made it safely back to Tobruk to fight again.

The decision to defend Tobruk and halt the retreat there was Wavell's. He had made this clear at a conference attended by Foreign Secretary Anthony Eden in Cairo on 6 April and, furthermore, had said at the conference that he intended to use troops earmarked for Greece to reinforce Tobruk.

The importance of making a stand at Tobruk was clear. It was important as a sally-port, from where the Allies could go out to attack the Germans and Italians. But, much more than this, possession of Tobruk meant that Rommel could not push forward into Egypt. One of the most significant statistics of the entire campaign was that the Axis forces in Libya needed about 50,000 tonnes of supplies each month if they were to remain in Cyrenaica and cross the frontier into Egypt. Through the port of Tripoli, which was the only Libyan port of any size in their possession, they could lift only 29,000 tonnes a month.

If they captured Tobruk, they could bring all the supplies they needed right up to their front line. For even if they had been able to increase the tonnage being handled by Tripoli, the line of supply from there to the eastern frontier of Cyrenaica was almost unmanageably long.

Tobruk, then, became as important to both sides as Malta. Both were a major thorn in the side of the Axis and both were vital to the Allied defence and offence in North Africa.

Churchill, who not infrequently encouraged soldiers and civilians alike to fight until they dropped, urged that Tobruk be held 'to the death without thought of retirement.' And for once the

Prime Minister and Wavell, who were not enamoured of each other, saw eye to eye.

Wavell had left the conference and flown straight to Tobruk to fill the gap left by the capture of Generals Neame and O'Connor. He appointed Major-General John Lavarack, an Australian who was commanding the 7th Division, as Commander-in-Chief, Cyrenaica Command, in place of Neame. And, at Wavell's suggestion, Lavarack named Morshead Commander of Tobruk Fortress, with the overriding order that, if possible, Tobruk was to be held for two months.

Wavell had arrived at Tobruk with Lavarack in the middle of a violent *khamsin*, the ochre dust turning the day to near-night. The RAF pilot managed to put them down safely on the sand, but it was another hour before the reception committee sent out to meet them could find them. Few who have not seen one at first hand can imagine the intensity and ferocity of the *khamsin*.

But in the afternoon there was nearly an incident with far more dire consequences. Wavell left in the early afternoon to fly back to Cairo, but the aircraft had to turn back with engine trouble and it was nearly dusk when they left again. After only a short time in the air the engine failed yet again and this time there was no chance of turning back to Tobruk. They put down in the desert in the darkness, and the plane was wrecked.

For six hours General Headquarters in Cairo feared that, as well as losing three of their generals to the Germans, they had now lost their Commander-in-Chief to the desert. But next morning a search patrol found Wavell and his pilot alive and well near Salum. Later that morning a small Lysander took him straight on to Cairo.

After the first glimpse of the enemy when the pursuing Germans and Italians had almost by accident come up against the Tobruk defences, the defenders inside the wire saw nothing of them for two days. They stood at their posts from first light, peering uncomfortably and painfully into the *khamsin* expecting the shape of an enemy tank to loom up over them at any moment, but all that came were a few stragglers making their way back to safety.

There were the inevitable post mortems at every level down to the youngest private. What had gone wrong, apart from the obvious disparity in the two forces and the brilliance of Rommel? Certainly the situation wasn't helped when Churchill did not withdraw his offer to Greece when he learned of the far greater threat in North Africa after the Africa Corps had arrived.

And what of Wavell as a commander? Rommel himself said that Wavell was the only British general 'who showed a touch of genius.' He had a brilliant background and had written a masterly paper defining his task as Commander-in-Chief. He had argued correctly that Germany would aim at domination of eastern and south-eastern Europe, whilst Italy strove to do the same in the Mediterranean and North Africa, her traditional areas of influence, and he was sure that the eastern Mediterranean would be the decisive theatre.

If not quite to the extent of Montgomery, who made a cult of never bothering himself with paper-work or of allowing a staff officer to come between himself and his men, Wavell certainly never cluttered up the major issues that he tackled by trying to do his own staff work. But he disapproved fervently of Churchill's continued attempts to interfere in what he considered to be his own responsibility, the disposal of his troops. He not only disapproved in principle, but he thought than many of Churchill's proposals were stupid and some positively dangerous.

It was inevitable, therefore, that the two men would not see eye to eye and from the writings of both of them, it is clear that this antipathy dated back to their first meeting. Wavell was not one of Churchill's generals and Churchill found that he did not like Wavell very much. He found him too cool, too unemotional and, unforgivably, too independent. He liked his generals to let him interfere.

Wavell had certainly given Churchill wrong advice when he had told him, even after learning of the arrival of Rommel and the Africa Corps in Tripolitania, that he did not believe that the Germans would do more than test the Allies at El Agheila and then possibly, if they met no resistance, push on to Agedabia where there was a useful airfield. In particular, he had not believed that they would attempt to seize Benghazi.

In hindsight, of course, the advice was wrong, but it was wrong only because he had not read Rommel correctly. His interpretation was exactly in accord with what the German High Command had decided. It had just never occurred to him that Rommel would simply disobey the High Command.

And even if his first enemies in North Africa were only Italians, for any commander with a force of just 36,000 men to rout an army of nearly 250,000, taking a vast number of them prisoner, was a remarkable achievement.

In the end, Wavell just asked his men to do too much. Had they been battle-hardened, it would have been an impossible task. As it was, they were green and had no chance of winning from the moment when Greece was given priority over North Africa and Hitler decided to send in the Africa Corps. What that humiliating experience did achieve, however, was that overnight these inexperienced men were exposed to fire and were tempered for the long ordeal that lay ahead of them in the Fortress of Tobruk.

When the 6th Australian Division had assaulted and captured Tobruk on the way east on 21 January, Morshead had just arrived in the Middle East from England. He spent several days after the assault inspecting the defences of the fortress which had been erected by the Italians, and getting a detailed picture of the terrain.

The perimeter of the Fortress was about 45 km in length and it ran in an arc round the city, with each end touching the coast. The two ends were about 27 km apart and the average distance of the perimeter from the town centre was approximately 14 km.

The harbour was the best in Italian North Africa, though it was cluttered now with the wreckage of several ships which had been sunk there. The town itself, before it had been laid waste, had been an attractive resort with wide, leafy streets and many large villas.

The main roads leading out of Tobruk were to Bardia and Egypt in the east; to Derna, Benghazi and Tripolitania in the west; and to El Adem in the south. There were, as well, several age-old tracks which reached out into the desert, sometimes disappearing altogether under the onslaught of the *khamsin*.

West of the town there was a plain, about 5 km wide, and on the southern edge of this plain there was the escarpment that climbed sharply up to a fairly flat ledge of land on the far side of which was another escarpment that dropped back to the desert. Standing on top of the plateau, looking south, the country was flat almost as far as the eye could see except at one point in the south-west where a hill known as Ras el Medauuar dominated the skyline. This hill was just inside the perimeter. In the east, the two escarpments came closer and closer together until they merged on the coast.

A number of *wadis* cut across the coastal plain on both sides of the harbour, deep chasms eroded into the rock. To the west the principal *wadi* was Sehel which was an enormous gorge, and to the east and only slightly smaller was Zeitun, then Weddan and Belgassem.

Sehel and Zeitun were formidable natural defences and were at either end of the perimeter. Weddan and Belgassem were outside the perimeter, Belgassem being some 2000 m outside.

The outer perimeter, constructed by the Italians, became known as the 'Red Line' and consisted of a minefield, then a deep anti-tank ditch carved into solid rock but not completed when the Italians were driven out, and inside that a box wire obstacle. Where this had not been completed, ordinary concertina barbed wire was used. The anti-tank ditch was intended eventually to join the Sehel *wadi* in the west and the Zeitun *wadi* in the east.

For the whole length of the wire, there were dog's-legs approximately every 750 m and in the apex of these a frontier post, typically containing three circular concrete weapon pits at ground level, connected by underground concrete passages which also led to bomb-proof sleeping, living and storage rooms.

They looked at first glance impressive and strong, but their layout meant that only a few people could actually fight at any one time in the weapon pits. If they were overcome, as they easily could be by tanks, all the other people in the post were helpless.

But the posts had good fields of fire and they could cover both sides of the dog's-leg. Around the pits was usually a ring of booby traps and between that and the perimeter wire at least two rows of anti-personnel mines.

About 500 m behind these forward posts and covering the gaps between each two of them, was a second row of similar posts. They were all numbered consecutively, the odd numbers being on the perimeter wire, the even numbers behind. The posts between Ras el Medauuar and the Sehel *wadi* had the prefix 'S' and those between the hill and the Zeitun *wadi* in the east had the prefix 'R'.

When Tobruk was occupied in January, the first priority was to strengthen the defences. The wire needed to be renewed in places, minefields put down where the anti-tank ditch had not been completed, and the roads entering the perimeter at either side, from Derna and Bardia, blown up. Road blocks were placed across the other roads and tracks coming into the perimeter and local defences improved, a hard and thankless task in ground where the rock was frequently less than 30 cm below the surface.

Morshead had expected to find an inner and shorter perimeter than the Red Line which he had intended to occupy as being much easier to defend with his small force. But it turned out to exist nowhere but in the fantasies of some intelligence officer. There were a few sangars (stone-built breastworks) and shallow weapon pits in the vicinity of the most likely approach areas that the British had been expected to take, but they were valueless.

The terrain was dry, unwelcoming desert. About the only thing that grew in any quantity was a stunted shrub known to the troops as camel-thorn because they were the only living thing that would touch it. Apart from a few fig trees near the wells, there were no trees and much of the ground was absolutely bare and devoid of life.

The entire country did not have one perennial river. The *wadis* filled with water during the flash-floods that followed the rains, but dried up as quickly and reverted almost at once to a dry bed or a small trickle. Around Barce the soil was light and fertile, but everywhere else in Cyrenaica there was nothing but the wind-eroded sand or the stony desert. Oil was still twelve years away from being discovered and Libya was as desperately poor then as it is bountifully rich today.

The fearful heat of the Sahara was moderated along the coast, but the days could still be broilingly hot. July and August were the hottest months with the temperature going up to an average 29°C and January and February were the coolest. On average only 30 cm of rain fell a year on Tobruk and when it did, the climate was cloyingly humid and enervating. Worst of all by far were the hot, arid winds that swept up from the Sahara, carrying with them vast clouds of dust and sand.

These *khamsins* could rage for days, but when the weather was clear, the early morning and evening could be very agreeable and the summer nights a delight. As the morning sun warmed the desert, a mirage would subtly change it. The colour and broad outline were unaltered, but features that before were sharp against the horizon were now shimmering as though seen through an out of focus lens.

If the effect was rather beautiful to most eyes, it was a menace to the artillery who could no longer range their guns accurately. You can't take aim at a mirage and if you fire at it, you don't see where your shots are landing. As a result, one of the regular events at the start and end of each day was a volley of artillery fire from both sides as they did their ranging.

The speed at which the Fortress was organised into a working base during the next month was remarkable. Two excellent water pumping stations which the Italians had mined but left only slightly damaged were repaired, one just outside the perimeter in the Sehel *wadi*, the other in the middle of the Fortress in the Auda *wadi*. The engineers who carried out this work also repaired the electrical power system and the bulk petrol storage depot.

In an effort to get rid of as many useless mouths as possible, Morshead arranged for 8000 of the 25,000 Italian prisoners to be shipped out. One of the bleak spots was that, in spite of all the efforts of Colonel Lloyd, Morshead's Chief of Staff, to secure the motor vehicle and tank spares that they desperately needed, nothing arrived. The best he could achieve was a vague assurance from AIF Headquarters in Alexandria that the problem would be resolved 'by shipment on the water from Australia'.

The Area Commander in Tobruk, Lt Colonel T. P. Cook, who was in charge of the base from the first day of the occupation, worked hard at trying to combat the low morale of many of the men there. Inevitably, among a force of men who had just been thrashed by a powerful enemy, rumours proliferated about what might or might not be going to happen.

There were stories of impending surrender, of German parachutists gathering in Sicily to land on the Fortress (which everybody knew wasn't really a fortress with high walls, a moat and a drawbridge), and of what the Germans might do to them when they were captured. Most of them were furphies, but most of them were also very undesirable among men who already expected the worst.

Cook decided that the best method of countering this kind of half-truth, and of feeding the men's imaginations with a little positive propaganda, was to publish the truth. So he found a former journalist working in the Army Service Corps, Melbourne-based Sergeant W. H. Williams, and told him to publish a news-sheet every day. It was known as the *Tobruk Truth* or *The Dinkum Oil*.

Williams drew heavily on transcripts of the BBC news, which most of the men did not hear for there were few short-wave radio sets. He coloured it with items of local interest, up-to-date information on what other units were doing, and a very watered-down account of what the Germans were doing.

The news-sheet, which had no breaks for paragraphs because white space was a waste of precious paper, was roneoed, on a captured Italian duplicator, as soon after midnight as possible so that it could be sent to every depot with the rations. In spite of a passing problem, when the duplicator was destroyed by a bomb blast, *The Dinkum Oil* came out right through the siege, reaching a circulation of 800 copies. Every unit and detachment received a copy, so that every man could read it and Williams, who was then 30, did most of the work single-handed.

Individual battalions and other units could also bring out their own newspaper and several did. The 2/24th Battalion, for example, produced the *Furphy Flyer* and the 2/48th the *48 News Sheet*. The *Furphy Flyer* had a style and content all its own. It tended to strike a personal note.

'Gentlemen do not refer to piss tins as such,' an editorial cautioned its readers, 'nor yet as urinals. They should please employ the correct military reference which is, "Urinals, desert-rose pattern, troops for the peeing into." '

Colonel Allen Spowers, the Battalion Commander, spoke the truth when he said at the *Flyer's* launching, 'The importance of the part played by the daily newspaper in our lives is only appreciated when we are compelled to do without one.' The task of producing it was given to the Intelligence Section which Spowers, a most popular commander, was quick to point out would never entitle them to claim that they were intelligent.

At a more ponderous level, a note of caution was officially included in the Divisional Commander's Orders of 9th Division. It read, 'During the past fortnight (i.e. at the beginning of April) Fifth Columnists have been active in spreading rumours calculated to cause alarm and despondency. Some of these have been of the usual defeatist nature while others have been of a more insidious type of "disappointment" rumour, or "flop" whisper.'

It was a curious extension of the phrase fifth columnist to use it to describe gloomy soldiers of one's own unit!

A little later, Brigadier George Wootten, commanding 18th Brigade, exhorted his commanding officers to try and foster a new fighting spirit among the men. 'All ranks must be filled with a feeling that as Australians they are better fighting men than the Germans and the Italians,' he urged.

It was easy enough for them to believe that they were superior to the Italians. Italian jokes, like the evergreen *Tales of Italian Heroism* with twenty blank pages, were legend. They all had a certain sameness to them, like this one borrowed verbatim from the *Furphy Flyer*.

'Tony, you're a parachute soldier, eh?' said the CO to the captured Iti. 'And you were dropped from the big new plane that just flew over?'

'Yessir,' nodded Tony. 'New typo plano. Carry 50 men, but only one parachutist.'

'And what,' asked the CO, 'are the other 49 for?'

'Wot you tink?' replied Tony. 'Why, they're needed to push out the parachutist!'

Not very subtle but sure to raise a very healthy belly laugh. It was much harder, though, to foster this feeling about the Germans. An army of good soldiers led by a good general who was actually respected by his enemies can very easily seem to be an army of better soldiers led by a better general. And the logical extension of that kind of negative reasoning is that soldiers come to think that they are inferior.

Morshead knew very well that the only sure way of countering this frame of mind was to make sure that his men took on the Germans on equal terms — and won.

The last place that Brigadier Wootten had expected to find himself with his 18th Brigade was in Tobruk and, indeed, when Morshead returned to Tobrul on 8 April he was just as surprised himself. But Wavell, having made the decision to hold out against the Axis in Tobruk, lost no time in bringing in the minimum number of reinforcements that he thought necessary.

He had decided that he required four infantry brigade groups plus a small task force, which in fact was all the tanks he could muster. As events proved, he was right, if only just. The garrison did all and more that he had dared hope of it, but there wasn't an ounce of safety margin.

At the same time as he made this decision, the 7th Division, still under General Lavarack before his appointment to command of Cyrenaica, was preparing to move to Greece from its camp in Palestine. In fact, Lavarack had already received his orders to move to Alexandria for embarkation.

As he passed through Cairo on 4 April, he had received a message from Wavell directing him to report to the Commander-in-Chief that evening. Wavell explained his dilemma and asked for Lavarack's opinion about the wisdom of sending his 18th Brigade, together with artillery and a Field Ambulance, to Tobruk.

Lavarack said later that there really wasn't much consultation, but that he had no option but to agree that the 8th Division, consisting of fellow Australians, needed help and that this couldn't be denied them. That same evening 18th Brigade received its orders to move to Tobruk the next morning instead of to Egypt. Part of the brigade went by road, but the majority travelled by ship.

Wootten was immediately appointed Commander of the entire Australian force in Tobruk and one of his battalion commanders, Lt Colonel J. E. G. Martin, took over as acting commander of the Brigade. Wootten decided that, with the number of troops he now had, he could occupy the whole perimeter, which had been impossible before the arrival of the 18th Brigade.

He placed the 24th Brigade in the western sector and the 18th Brigade in the east, both with two battalions on the perimeter and one in reserve. And this was their position when the other Australians began to arrive back at Tobruk ahead of the Germans.

Blamey, the Australian GOC, was predictably furious, and not least because he hadn't been consulted. But Wavell was perfectly aware of what his reaction would be whether he consulted him or not, so there seemed no point. Instead, he cabled the Chief of the Australian General Staff, General Sturdee, with his intentions and told him that he was keeping Blamey in touch with the situation. In fact he did nothing of the sort and Blamey knew nothing about the move until he heard it from Australia.

The Australian Government said that it was 'greatly concerned and unwilling' and Blamey said that the retention of Libya was not vital to the defence of Egypt, anyway, however much its loss might affect British prestige. He added that the Expeditionary Force in Greece would be in great peril if it was weakened in this way by the removal of the 18th Brigade.

Wavell was sympathetic but unmoved and he rubbed salt into the wound by telling Blamey that he might well have to take the rest of the division away as well if the situation did not improve. The very next day came news that the situation was far worse. The Germans had advanced into Greece, Mechili had been overrun, the three generals captured, and the 9th Division was on the run in front of the Germans.

It was on the following day that Lavarack was appointed to succeed Neame and on that same day, the remainder of the 7th Division was ordered to Mersa Matruh to defend the Egyptian and Libyan frontier and, if necessary, Egypt itself. The 6th British Division, which was being trained for a landing on Rhodes in the Greek islands, was also sent to the Western Desert. It was because of this preponderance of Australian troops that Lavarack, an Australian, was given command. It was an inflexible rule — as Morshead and Lavarack were later to find to their cost — that Dominion officers were never given the highest command of units of other than their own men.

Lavarack was given pencilled instructions by Wavell who told him that his main task was to hold the enemy's advance at Tobruk 'in order to give time for the assembly of reinforcements, especially of armoured troops, for the defence of Egypt.'

He was to prepare a plan for withdrawl from Tobruk, if his position became untenable, both by land and sea; and his defence was to be as mobile as possible. He was to take 'any opportunity of hindering the enemy's concentration by offensive action.'

It Wavell's reluctance to ask Blamey for his opinion of transferring the Australians to Tobruk and the desert was understandable, what seemed to be quite unforgivable was that he had also made no attempt to advise the Australian Government of the very great danger the Australians in Cyrenaica were facing when Rommel attacked. Both Wavell and Churchill seem to have been too preoccupied with Greece. Even more inexplicable was that Blamey, too, neglected to tell the Australian War Cabinet, apparently because he also could think only of Greece.

Wavell's concept was to use the garrison force of Australians to defend the Fortress, and the mobile forces, mainly the 3rd Indian Motor Brigade (whose patrol had tangled with the German patrol in the desert) and reinforcements from the British 7th Armoured Division to harass the enemy in the desert.

When virtually all that remained of 9th Division was back inside the Tobruk perimeter (the great majority of the division did eventually get back) Lavarack reallocated the positions on the perimeter. The 18th Brigade was put into reserve for counter-attack duties and the whole of the perimeter was now guarded by the 9th Division.

On his first evening a brief and abortive attempt was made by a patrol of 20th Brigade to rescue the three generals taken at Mechili during the disorganised retreat. Reports had come in with some stragglers that they were being held in a *wadi* near Mechili and Morshead instructed the King's Dragoon Guards to provide the patrol with an escort of four armoured cars in spite of their commanding officer's protests that it was a gross misuse of them. Confined to roads at night, he complained, they were sitting ducks for anyone who chose to shoot at them.

In the end the patrol left late, with the armoured cars, but it was so delayed by demolition work that the Sappers had carried out the day before at Gazala that there was no possibility of them being able to return to Tobruk before daylight. The rescue attempt was abandoned.

On 9th April 300 vehicles, including tanks, armoured cars and trucks, were reported to be approaching Tobruk from the west while still more columns were setting out from Mechili. By early afternoon they were at Acroma, less than 30 km from Tobruk but only half that distance from the perimeter and just out of range of the British guns.

Towards dusk, an enemy gun opened up lightly on the 26th Brigade, and for most of the men who had remained in the Fortress and not gone forward, it was their first taste of battle fire. Enemy vehicles then appeared over the skyline but hurriedly withdrew when they were shelled by Allied artillery.

At 4 a.m. on 10 April, the last unit to return to Tobruk, the 2/48th Battalion, came into the perimeter and the Germans crept closer, widening their net around the Fortress. The siege of Tobruk had begun.

The Fierce Onslaught

Rommel had not slackened the speed of his advance and he constantly urged his columns on, cursing them when they lost their direction or slowed down, praising them when they kept up with his exhausting pace. He needed not only to surround and then attack Tobruk while morale inside the perimeter was still low but to go past the Fortress and defeat any reserves being brought forward from Egypt before they reached Tobruk.

He could not attack Egypt without his main force, but for that he had to have a secure supply position; and for that in turn, he needed to capture Tobruk. That he made no attempt to do more than harass the defenders for three days was in large part due to the absurd situation that he still had no map of the defences. Not one of the Italians under his command could find one.

However, nobody inside the perimeter on 11 and 12 April had any illusions — the German attack was imminent. Outside the wire, at dark, there was constant noise of vehicles moving and men digging in. A party of Italian engineers, equipped to break through the wire, was found in the anti-tank ditch. And a spotter plane that went out at last light reported the arrival of yet more columns from the south-west.

The fear that there were still enemy inside the compound who would come out and cause havoc as soon as the German attack began, seemed to have been confirmed when a group of Italians was discovered living in caves on the escarpment. The caves contained clothes, blankets and rations for six weeks, but no arms or radio for signalling to their colleagues outside the wire. Their story was that they were medical orderlies who had not been noticed when the other 25,000 Italians surrendered, and there was no reason to disbelieve them.

None the less, it caused concern, and warnings were issued that the enemy might try to penetrate the perimeter fence, perhaps wearing British or Australian uniforms and driving captured vehicles. (Throughout the campaign both sides made extensive use of each other's captured vehicles, sometimes hardly bothering to remove the old markings.)

Early Intelligence reports from 9th Division suggested that the enemy was using this transport for 'gangster warfare', but they didn't elaborate. And there were many mistakes made about German uniforms, in particular, which sometimes brought Germans close to being shot for dressing as British soldiers and so technically being spies.

In Crete, for example, it was widely reported that the Germans were wearing New Zealand battledress when, in fact, they were wearing a new German tropical kit. Standing orders for dealing with Germans genuinely found to be wearing an Allied uniform were uncompromisingly specific: 'Any such persons should be sent to this Headquarters before being shot.'

There were constant reminders to treat every stranger with suspicion, whether he wore a uniform or not. 'There is a strong tendency to assume that once people are inside a HQ or other military area, they are there on legitimate business,' an Intelligence report warned officers. 'This is NOT necessarily the case. Any stranger, whether in uniform or plain clothes, should be treated with definite suspicion.'

Then it was found that native workmen were turning up wearing odd items of Allied uniform that had been thrown away by their owners or by the stores. Weeks went by before it occurred to anyone that they could be invaluable to any prisoner-of-war wanting to escape, or to an enemy wanting to get in wearing disguise. Belatedly the practice was stopped.

The Germans appeared to have a wider range of transport than the Allies. Apart from their tanks and other AFVs, they used what looked like a heavy open touring car with two axles at the rear. It appeared to carry no armour, but a machine gun was mounted on a pillar in the back. The car travelled at considerable speed.

There were also a number of small two-seater cars, apparently staff cars, which carried no mounted weapons. The occupants were armed with a rifle and a pistol and if there was an officer he carried a sub-machine-gun. Like captured British lorries, they usually flew a small white flag with a red swastika.

The noise of activity outside the wire on the night of the 11th reached such a level that soon after 11 p.m. Lavarack became convinced that the attack would come at dawn. He ordered Wootten to move his 18th Brigade, which was in reserve, to the junction of the Bardia and El Adem roads in readiness. At 3 a.m. the men of the 18th were climbing into their trucks, and by first light they were in position, peering anxiously through a light *khamsin* in what they imagined was the direction of the enemy.

As the dust died down, 2/17th Battalion, who were to the south of the 18th Brigade, could clearly see the enemy dug in less than 400 m from the perimeter, in front of a company commanded by Captain J. W. Balfe who was to see a lot of fighting before the next two days were over. Then some gunners arrived and began digging seven anti-tank guns in near the perimeter, with the enemy sniping at them from time to time.

As the morning wore on, movement anywhere near the wire became very hazardous as the enemy stepped up its machine gun and mortar fire, but a party went out from post R35 under cover from a Bren gun and, lying on their backs under the fence, carried out urgent repairs to the wire.

By mid-morning it was clear that the attack was not as imminent as Lavarack had feared (Rommel had still not received his maps) and the 18th Brigade was withdrawn into reserve again.

From that time, almost the only aircraft they saw over Tobruk, apart from the small local reconnaisance planes, were enemy ones. The RAF, with few fighters to start with and driven as they had been out of one airfield after another, were in no position to retaliate over the desert. No 73 (Fighter) Squadron and No 6 Squadron, both of the RAF, were still valiantly operating from the small Tobruk airfield in the south of the Fortress, but they had only twelve Hurricanes and had been told there would be no replacements. They answered every call for help, but in the face of an overwhelmingly superior enemy air force their effective power was diminishing daily.

After lunch on 12 April, the ships in the harbour were attacked by 15 dive-bombers, but anti-aircraft fire was so accurate that three were shot down and none of the ships was damaged.

Enemy tanks made a few incursions towards the wire and were driven off and then, when the *khamsin* started to blow up in the late afternoon, they advanced under cover of the dust towards R33 and R35. Post R32, behind the perimeter, at once opened fire and the enemy went to ground about 500 m from the wire, but then began to advance again.

Once more they were shelled and were broken up, and many were seen to take cover in the anti-tank ditch just on the other side of the wire. One group, however, more daring than the rest, was clearly about to press home an attack on R33. They opened fire, but got back more than they gave from the section in the post, ably led by former Manly milkman Lance-Corporal A. E. Dunbar, who returned such withering fire that the enemy beat a hasty retreat. Dunbar was awarded the Military Medal.

At 4 p.m. six RAF bombers came over and, at Lavarack's request and to the delight of the defenders, bombed about sixty tanks and some other vehicles which were visible even through the dust near the El Adem Road.

It was an untidy day for both sides, but if Rommel never intended to do more than harass them, the defending troops did not know that and it did untold good to their morale to think that for the first time they had found the measure of the Germans.

That night there was a nearly full moon which bathed the desert in a soft light. It gave the defenders standing to in their positions an excellent view of anything moving on the other side of the wire. At about 10 p.m. Captain Balfe saw two groups of vehicles crossing his front, comprising twenty-nine lorries filled with troops and twelve vehicles which appeared to be pulling guns.

Balfe lost no time in positioning himself in the artillery observation post at R32 and then he personally directed a moonlight strike by the guns against the enemy. He was then only twenty-nine, a company secretary from the Queensland town of Charters Towers, but few men in the Fortress so deserved the Military Cross that he was later awarded for his bravery and example.

At one minute past midnight on 14 April there was a change of command that hardly affected the men on the perimeter. The defending force for Egypt was so spread out, from Tobruk to the Canal, that it made sense for it to be under a single command and so a Western Desert Headquarters was formed out of the old Cyrenaica Command of General Lavarack. But it did not include Tobruk Fortress which was deliberately kept outside the new set-up with Morshead virtually answerable to no one outside his perimeter. The Cruiser tanks inside the perimeter were needed on the Egyptian frontier, but Morshead had no intention of parting with them until he had at least eight of the 'I' (for Infantry) tanks that had been promised to him. Without them he had no chance of mounting the mobile offensive patrols which Wavell had said were almost as important a role for Tobruk's garrison as the defence of the Fortress.

On the 12th, Rommel finally got the maps that he needed. There were only two of them and Rommel gave one to General Streich commanding the 5th Light Division. From the maps they were at last able to plan an accurate assault plan and on Sunday 13 April, Easter Day, they were finally ready to go.

There were now Germans completely surrounding Tobruk and the plan was for Streich and his division to mount the main assault in the south, breaching the wire on the evening of 13 April. Another division would cause a diversion in the west to pin down any forces there; and in the early hours of the 14th, the main force would push through this bridgehead and launch a dawn attack in the direction of the harbour.

At about 3 p.m. on the afternoon of the 11th, 2/13th and 2/17th Battalions had a dramatic baptism by fire. The 2/13th and the British machine-gunners supporting them had forced to ground some infantry who approached within 400 m of the wire near their front. But then seven tanks appeared directly in front of post R31 and advanced through the fire.

Fifteen minutes later, artillery observers reported that more infantry were advancing towards 2/17th positions near R33. Again the artillery stopped them, but this time twenty tanks, seeming to ignore the barrage, came straight up to the perimeter. They were followed by another wave of twenty and then a third and, finally, a smaller group of ten. When all seventy tanks were lined up along the anti-tank ditch, they opened fire simultaneously on the 2/17th.

They were a mixed bag, some were light Italian tanks and Italian M13s, but others were big German Mk IVs, each with a huge 73-mm gun. The Allies did not have a single anti-tank gun between them in those positions, but they blazed away with anti-tank rifles, bren-guns and rifles. What the enemy clearly didn't know was that the minefield at that point in the perimeter, chosen because the anti-tank ditch was shallow and had not been properly completed, was only temporary and they could have crossed it with minimal casualties. Instead, after bombarding the 2/17th, they turned their attention on the 2/13th who were next in line to the east and astride the El Adem road inside the perimeter.

More infantry came and were repulsed and the fighting only stopped at dusk, leaving the Australians exhausted and exhilarated.

Rommel's eastwards thrust, meanwhile, pushing forward towards the Egyptian frontier, was approaching Fort Capuzzo. There was a brief skirmish with Allied armoured cars which captured German prisoners and extracted the information that a battalion was in the area, but it was not enough even to hold up the Germans.

The border town of Salum stands on a bay of the same name at the foot of a steep escarpment. The road winds up this escarpment, through the Halfaya Pass, to the plateau where the Salum Barracks stood guard over the town below.

At dawn the next day the defending troops, a company of the Durham Light Infantry positioned on the escarpment, withdrew having fired some ineffectual demolition charges in the pass behind them. They caused the Germans no trouble and by 2 p.m. Capuzzo had been captured. The Allied oiled the wells before they left. Two hours later, the Germans were in the Salum Barracks. There, for the moment, Rommel was content to wait. He had tested the water in Egypt and, for the time being, that was sufficient. Wavell watched with growing concern.

Meanwhile, back at Tobruk, the Axis force was flexing its muscles preparing for the battle that would yield them the vital fortress and prepare the ground for the final push into Egypt and eventual domination of the whole of North Africa and the Western Desert.

Easter morning began with deceptive calm. Soon after sun-up a German staff car, escorted by motor cyclists, arrived directly in front of Captain Balfe and 2/17th Battalion. An officer got out of the car and it appeared as though a headquarters was being set up. The Allied artillery immediately began to shell it and the anti-tank gunners optimistically opened up at extreme range on the staff car. German activity stopped abruptly.

Soon afterwards a Heinkel flew low over the perimeter and was greeted with a hail of small arms fire. Later again other aircraft came over and dropped leaflets inviting the British and Australians to surrender. 'Strong German forces have already surrounded Tobruk,' it said in large capital letters, 'and it is useless to try and escape. Remember Mekili (Mechili). Our dive-bombers and Stukas are awaiting your ships which are lying in Tobruk.'

The Allies were to come out waving white handkerchiefs, to which Morshead commented, in his report of the incident, with a rare glimpse of humour, that because of the prevailing dust and of the need to ration water for essential purposes, no white handkerchiefs were available.

At both ends of the sector, trucks, probably captured from the British at Mechili or in the desert, drove up to the perimeter wire. The one in the eastern sector drove off as soon as it was fired on, but in the west 2/48th Battalion laid a trap and captured the truck and its crew. In the back, realising the worst fears of Intelligence officers, were two motor-cycles and an Australian and Indian uniform. Several other vehicles and crews were captured by the 2/48th in the same way.

The Germans next brought up infantry in lorries which stopped about 4000 m from the southern perimeter. Men got out, seemingly oblivious of the enemy watching them closely, until a few well-placed rounds from the British artillery sent them scampering in every direction.

Then, under intense fire, small detachments were brought even closer to the wire, and when they were no more than 1500 m away, they set up machine guns which immediately began to fire on the nearest posts and kept up their fire whenever anything moved.

Untroubled by the anti-aircraft fire, two enemy reconnaisance aircraft cruised up and down the lines, apparently studying the ground defences carefully. They paid particular attention to the area around the 2/17th and if its commanding officer, Colonel J. W. Crawford, felt a mounting sense of excitement, it was because his instinct had been right. He was to bear the brunt of the attack.

Crawford was not a professional soldier although anything military had been his abiding interest since school days. At Sydney University he had risen to command the University Regiment at the relatively young age of 34. Now, at 4 p.m., he moved his reserve company up behind Balfe's company, which was holding posts R30 to R35.

The German timetable showed the attack due to start at 5 p.m. on Easter Day and precisely on five, Balfe's company found itself being heavily bombarded by Italian artillery, followed by a torrent of small arms fire. When they looked cautiously through the barbed wire, they saw enemy infantry coming closer, accompanied by a few tanks, until it was stopped by deadly fire from their own artillery behind them.

That it was only a temporary lull was confirmed by the evening reconnaissance plane which returned to report 300 vehicles on the El Adem road to the south. As darkness fell two German tanks drove slowly along the far side of the anti-tank ditch, apparently looking for a gap in the wire that they expected to find.

A signal arrived from Wavell for all ranks. 'I am glad that I have at this crisis such stout-hearted and magnificent troops in Tobruk. Am very heartened by what I have heard of their fighting spirit and conduct during these operations. I know I can count on you to hold Tobruk to the end. My best wishes to you all.'

Holding Tobruk 'to the end' was an unfortunate choice of phrase for men who were expecting to be overrun before daylight came round again. And the 2/17th Battalion felt far from stout-hearted as they waited to take the brunt of the attack.

The anti-tank ditch, in the sector which Rommel had chosen for the breach, was only about 75 mm deep in front of R33, while elsewhere at that part of the perimeter it was about 3.6 m deep. What he only found out later was that between R27 and R29 there were no tank traps at all and a breach there would have given him almost direct access to the vital Pilastrino Ridge and to Fort Pilastrino, where Morshead had established his headquarters in an old Italian fortress. But he had selected the El Adem road as the axis of his advance and the area of the wire near R33, some 4 km west of the road, as the place where the breach would actually be made. His engineers had informed him that the anti-tank ditch was shallow at this point and the minefield would be cleared before the advance began.

From inside the Fortress patrols went out all that night, locating enemy positions, and attempting to bring in prisoners to gain information. Many succeeded, some did not. A platoon from the 2/43rd, who were on the far right of the perimeter between the coast and the Bardia Road, put on soft hats and sandshoes and went out under cover of darkness to surprise the enemy in the Belgassem *wadi*. Instead, they were surprised themselves and mown down by machine-gun and mortar fire. Five men were lost and five more were seriously wounded.

The 2/17th in the south was more successful and two patrols each brought in a German prisoner. (German prisoners had more reliable information than the Italians, but were more reluctant to part with it than the Italians who usually didn't stop talking.)

What followed in the next twenty-four hours was perhaps the turning point in the entire North African campaign. The battle gave neither side very tangible advantage, the Germans and Italians least of all; but it established in the minds of the defenders that the Germans weren't invincible. From that day there was a new hope, a new confidence, and without that the Allies would never have sustained the siege of Tobruk.

Rommel had timed the main breach to begin just before dawn. First, though, he needed the nearest strong point, post R33, neutralised and, at 11 p.m., thirty of his infantrymen, heavily armed with field guns, mortar and eight machine guns, dug under the wire about 100 m east of the post. Then they turned all their fire on the post.

By all the rules of warfare, they should have swamped it within minutes, but that didn't take account of the determination of the men in the post and particularly their leader, a 24-year-old commercial traveller in peacetime, Lieutenant F. A. Mackell.

Mackell had seen the Germans coming under the wire and knew what to expect. For a short time, he returned fire for fire, but this was clearly not going to dislodge the enemy. So, calling for covering fire, he led Corporal J. H. Edmondson and five other men out of the post to the north intending to come round on the Germans' flank.

The enemy saw them almost immediately and turned their fire on them, but the party was still able to get into position for an assault without injury. What followed was graphically described later by Mackell to war correspondent Chester Wilmot.

Mackell had arranged for his men back in the post to stop firing at a given moment and to begin shouting and yelling at the tops of their voices to confuse the enemy, while he and his party went in, shouting as loudly, with their bayonets fixed. The plan worked.

'It's amazing that we weren't all hit,' Mackell recalled afterwards. 'As we ran we threw our grenades and when they burst the German fire stopped. But already Jack Edmondson had been seriously wounded by a burst from the machine gun that had got him in the stomach and he'd also been hit in the neck. Still he ran on and before the Germans could open up again, we were into them.'

The Germans dropped their weapons and fled, some running straight into the barbed wire in their panic. They were pursued by the Australians, still shouting like wild men, and felt the cold steel of their bayonets.

Mackell went on, 'In spite of his wounds, Jack Edmondson was magnificent. As the Germans scattered, he chased them and killed at least two. By this time I was in difficulties, wrestling with one German on the ground while another was coming straight for me with a pistol.

'I called out, "Jack!", and from about fifteen yards away Edmondson ran to help me and bayonetted both Germans.'

Meanwhile the other members of the patrol were still piercing the Germans with their bayonets and Mackell, back on his feet, broke his bayonet on one German and then clubbed another with the butt. Edmondson fought on, in spite of his grievous wounds, until he could no longer stand.

Twelve Germans were dead, one was a prisoner and the rest had fled, many of them injured. His friends helped Jack Edmondson, who had been a farmer until he volunteered, back to the post and cared for him as well as they could, but the next morning he died. For his extraordinary bravery he was posthumously awarded the Victoria Cross, the first Australian to be awarded that decoration in World War II.

Mackell's night, however, was far from ended. Half an hour after midnight a German tank approached the proposed point of the breach, appeared to study it carefully and then withdrew. From post R33 the Australians could see in the moonlight that the mines had been lifted and neatly stacked on either side of the intended gap, but the ditch was still unbreached.

At 2.30 a.m. 200 infantry appeared out of the darkness and broke through the wire near R33. They then fanned out for several hundred metres inside the perimeter. From inside his post Mackell immediately called by Very light for artillery fire and it came within moments, accurate and heavy. Posts in the area joined in with small arms fire and to their delight they saw ambulances coming close to the wire. But the Germans had not been dislodged and they remained under cover, to be dealt with later.

For his part in the night's resistance, Mackell was awarded the Military Cross. He had delayed and upset Rommel's advance and he had been an inspiration to every other Australian in the Fortress.

Rommel's plan was for thirty-eight tanks of his 5th Armoured Regiment to keep heading north after the break-in was made, followed by a machine-gun battalion. After penetrating for 3.5 km, the leading tank battalion was to drive on to Tobruk, while the second battalion would 'pursue the retreating enemy' westwards. The wishful words were Rommel's.

The breach got off to an unfortunate start. Because the area of fence near post R33 had been selected, the tanks had to drive some way from the El Adem road and the officer detailed to guide them lost his way and took them too far to the east. Any hope of surprise was lost as the tanks doubled back looking for the right place. There appeared in the moonlight to be about forty of them.

As the moment for the break-in came closer, the enemy artillery opened up on the Garrison's defences, using for the first time 88-mm anti-aircraft guns as field artillery. The shells burst in the air over the heads of the defenders, making it a devastating weapon.

At exactly 5.20 a.m. the first tanks suddenly turned and dashed for the wire, passing through a gap that had been blown near Mackell's post R33. They headed straight for Company Headquarters in R32. There were fifteen tanks in this first wave, some of them pulling anti-aircraft and anti-tank guns, and they stopped almost on top of Captain Balfe's Headquarters.

Behind each tank, or riding on it, were between fifteen and

twenty infantry and these dropped behind as soon as they were inside the perimeter. The Allied infantry had been ordered to hold its fire until the tanks were safely past but then to open up on the infantrymen who followed; and this was exactly what they did.

Meanwhile, Balfe, with fifteen tanks sitting there, ordered the artillery to bring down fire on his own position, praying that the post was strongly enough fortified to withstand the attack. The artillery shortened its range and its fire landed on target, killing or wounding most of the machine-gunners who were still riding on the tanks and scattering the infantry in disarray. The tanks moved on without them and the posts intensified their fire on the foot soldiers who were now running to get back through the wire.

Just one group did not panic, and it established itself in a ruined house behind Balfe's headquarters, and in some sangars that had been left by the Italians.

The tanks turned right and headed back towards the El Adem road still, of course, inside the perimeter. Then they turned northeast, parallel to the road, and finally came to a stop facing north and waited for the dawn.

The artillery fired at them relentlessly while the Australians in the posts near the perimeter gaps poured steady fire at any unarmoured enemy who were rash enough to attempt a break-through. They shot many of them.

At dawn the fire increased in intensity. Near Balfe's headquarters, the Germans started firing three of their anti-tank guns and a small gun until they were picked off one by one by Australian snipers and silenced. Lieutenant W. B. A Geikie, (a Sydney solicitor in peacetime) who had led one of the successful patrols the previous day which had brought in the two German prisoners, personally killed four of the Germans.

So far the fight was going well for the Allies, but Rommel didn't delay before bringing up his big guns. As usual he was conducting the attack personally from a position not far from the perimeter.

The Australians watched in astonishment as huge, long-barrelled 88-mm guns, which they had never seen before, were dragged forward and positioned near the gap beside more conventional 75-mm field guns. However, before the Germans could even use them the Australians had despatched their crews in the same way as they had dealt with the anti-tank gunners. Enemy machine-gun posts inside the perimeter, established in the night, could also be picked out as the sun came up, and these too were subdued.

As soon as Lavarack learned of the German penetration, he had sought reinforcements from Morshead who immediately ordered the two Cruiser squadrons of the 1st Royal Tank Regiment to attack the enemy tanks which were now parked near the El Adem road inside the perimeter. As the squadrons approached the enemy came under spirited fire from the artillery and broke away from the huddle they had kept in since their arrival. In their worst moment, though, they could not have been prepared for what followed.

A troop of the 3rd Royal Horse Artillery worked its way round to the flank of the enemy tanks and engaged them in a cheeky, running fight. Then other guns joined in until seventeen of the enemy had been knocked out.

The others continued to move forward in bounds, advancing under intense fire on a troop of the 1st RHA. The gunners had no armour-piercing shells, but at 600 m their 25-pounders were just as deadly. Firing over open sights, the artillery poured shells into the exposed hulls of the tanks and left five more burning. The turret of a huge, 22-ton Mark IV tank, probably containing the Battalion Commander, was blown clean off.

The 11/5th Armoured Battalion which had been leading the advance suddenly stopped, turned in its tracks and headed back towards the perimeter — straight into the 1/5th Battalion which was just behind it. There was a terrible grinding of crashing metal and, to the cheers of the gunners, the tanks tried to extricate themselves from the mess while the 25-pounders kept pouring shells relentlessly into them.

There was pandemonium as the battle reached its crisis. The artillery were superb, standing to their guns against a seemingly relentless German advance. Many of their men died at their posts. One troop alone, Chestnut Troop of A/E Battery, had five of its members killed and three wounded, including both the officers at the guns.

As the tanks looked frantically for somewhere to go, the Allied Cruisers lumbered into action, hurling their fire from a range of 1.5 km and then beginning to close. They had intended to make a surprise move with the sun behind them, but there was no sun, only a thick layer of cloud at 1200 m. So heavy was the artillery attack, however, (the German tanks were now being attacked simultaneously by guns of the 1st, 3rd, 104th and 107th Royal Horse Artillery and 2/3rd Anti-Tank Regiment!) that they were not as heavily counter-attacked as they had expected.

While all was bedlam on the ground, the few indefatigable Hurricanes of the RAF fought spectacular dogfights over the battlefield. They destroyed four enemy planes and almost lost one of their own number when it was fired on by Allied anti-aircraft guns on the ground. While the pilot tried frantically to signal their mistake, an enemy aircraft dived in and succeeded where the anti-aircraft gunners had failed. Hurricane and pilot went into the desert.

Meanwhile the gunners could hear the sound of some fifty bombers approaching through their listening instruments. They were still some distance away, but there could be little doubt that their purpose was to soften up the town itself ready for an Axis occupation.

An urgent task for Colonel Crawford now was to silence the enemy who were entrenched in the deserted house behind Balfe's Company headquarters, from where they were causing a great deal of damage. He selected two platoons for the task and two sections of these made the first approach up to the house. The sections were led by a former bank clerk, Sergeant R. McElroy, a brave man who was later commissioned in the field after being awarded the Military Medal for this assignment, only to be killed in action eighteen months later.

The Germans in the house pretended to be Australians and called out in English in answer to another sergeant. When he approached the house, they shot him dead. Immediately McElroy led a charge against the house from 50 m in front of it hurling their grenades as they went, using the bayonet freely on any German who was slow to surrender. They killed eighteen and took another eighteen prisoner.

By now the predicament of the German tanks was serious and they were clearly trying to get out in any way they could. All around them were infantry, hoping for protection in the lee of the tanks as they passed through the wire. But they found no comfort there. Instead, they were stuck between the relentless guns of the artillery and the tanks, one after another of which was crippled.

Still the surviving tanks headed back towards the wire, but just when they believed that they were clear of the onslaught from 'J' Battery of the 3rd RHA, which had been causing them so much damage, they came within range of the 9th Battery of the 2/3rd Anti-Tank Regiment, which probably accounted for another eight tanks.

There were remarkable stories of individual bravery, as of the gunner in a three-man anti-tank gun crew who found himself the sole survivor of a machine-gun attack from a nearby German position. Although seriously wounded, he took over the gun himself and continued firing it ceaselessly until the machine gun fire ignited his ammunition and he was wounded again by the explosion and disabled. He was dragged to safety by a bombardier and survived.

As the escaping tanks neared the wire German infantry jumped on them for a ride back to safety. So fast were the tanks going that they caught a number of Australians, who were mopping up, out in the open. They had forced some of the men to surrender when two of the posts saw what was happening and opened up with fierce bren gun fire on the tanks, forcing the crews to pull in their heads and close up the tanks.

The Australians dived for cover and immediately in turn began firing on the German infantry on the backs of the tanks, forcing them, too, to run for cover. In the area around the gap there was a great pall of dust and dirt and into this the Allies continued to fire indiscriminately with everything at their disposal. Many German infantry were shot as they rushed past and many more were captured later where they had taken cover in the anti-tank ditches. There were reports of grenades being thrown in on top of others who were hiding in the ditches waiting for an opportunity to come out and surrender.

By 7.30 a.m. the Germans were beaten and at that moment the Stuka dive-bombers which the artillery had heard, arrived (though forty of them, not fifty). It was the time when Rommel had forecast that his leading victorious tank battalion would be approaching the town. Six of the German aircraft were destroyed, two by the Hurricanes, the others by anti-aircraft fire.

The Australians wanted to chase the German infantry right out through the gap and into the desert, but they were ordered to stay inside the perimeter and not risk themselves needlessly. By 8.30 a.m. the battle was over and the last of the tanks, which had not panicked, were disappearing into the distance, dragging behind them the big guns which they had stopped to pick up as they went through the gap.

At 1000 m, however, the artillery gave them a parting barrage which was so accurate that the tanks unhitched the guns and departed swiftly.

Rommel had timed a second attack to start at 6 p.m., to follow up what he never doubted would be the success of the first one. This was cancelled. Inside the battlefield alone there were 150 German dead and 250 prisoners; the Garrison's casualties were twenty-six dead and sixty-four wounded.

In an attempt to rescue the 8th Machine Gun Battalion, which was reported to be still holding out inside the perimeter, Rommel ordered a division of the Italian Army through a gap in the western sector. He ordered the Ariete Division to move into position in front of the perimeter wire in the evening ready to launch the attack after dark. The Italians found themselves under fire long before it was time to go through the wire and, almost to a man, they turned tail and fled.

The Allies had considerable mopping up to do in the perimeter for there were pockets of the enemy in many places. It was carried out systematically and cautiously and many Germans were killed or captured with very little loss to the Allies.

The reception that they received from the British and the Australians had left the Germans stunned. Colonel Friedrich Olbrich, the commander of the German armour, wrote in his battle report that Intelligence had told him that 'the enemy would retire immediately on the approach of German tanks'.

'They gave out before the attack', he went on, 'that the enemy was exhausted, that his artillery was extremely weak and that his morale had become very low. Before the beginning of the attack, the regiment had not the slightest idea of the well-designed and executed defences of the enemy, nor of a single battery position or the terrific number of anti-tank guns. Also it was not known that he had heavy tanks'.

If there was implied criticism in Olbrich's report that Rommel had sent them in without proper preparation, it did not save him from a tongue-lashing from the Desert Commander. Both he and his superior, General Streich, the commander of the 5th Light Division, were bitterly chastised for leaving the infantry in the lurch when they made their escape through the wire.

Three months later Rommel found an opportunity to get rid of Streich and one of the reasons that he gave was that Streich had refused an order to go back through the wire and rescue the infantry who were still trapped there.

The truth of the matter, however unpalatable for Rommel to swallow, was that when victory was not handed to them on a plate, the Germans lost their nerve. He had grossly miscalculated the strength of the Allies and he had wrongly assumed, as Olbrich had been told, that opposition would crumble as soon as the tanks burst through. Tactically, the most important failure by the Germans was that the assault forces did not reinforce the bridgehead immediately.

But the most significant factor in the whole victory was the new spirit and courage of the Australians in the forward posts and the artillery behind them. Never again would they seriously believe that they were basically inferior to the Germans or that the Germans were unbeatable on the battlefield.

Lavarack was still basking in the pleasure of the victory when he received a message from Wavell that he was to be relieved of his Cyrenaica Command. The command itself was to be merged into the Western Desert Force and, as that consisted of substantial numbers of British troops, Lavarack as an Australian, no matter what his talents, could not have command over them. Instead he was demoted to command of the 7th Australian Division, his old command, which now did not even have its 18th Brigade.

It was a humiliating slight for a very able soldier who had been ousted as Chief of the Australian General Staff in 1939 and had then seen Blamey given command of the AIF, a job to which he had aspired himself.

But nothing, apart from the sadness of friends lost and injured in the battle, was going to spoil the moment for the defenders of Tobruk. They had been told that they could resist a major German offensive and though many of them were novices to the battlefield and most would have thought secretly that it wasn't really possible, they had succeeded. It was a sweet victory indeed.

The once elegant Piazza Benito Mussolini, Tobruk, after the Allied occupation. ▶ (5416)

▲ Australian infantrymen on the heights overlooking Tobruk. (5603)
◀ Hordes of Italian prisoners cluttered up the fortress. (5595)
▼ Australian troops advancing on Italian positions at Tobruk. In the background, the Italian cruiser *San Giorgio* burns. (5399)

▲ General Sir Archibald Wavell with Australian 6th Division Commander, Major-General Iven Mackay, after the capture of Tobruk. (5633)

◀ Major-General Leslie Morshead. (21078)

▲ Lieutenant-General Stanley Savige with Major Hurley and Lt. Colonel J. C. (Jock) Campbell in Tobruk. (5660)
◀ The church at Tobruk, unmarked by the Allied bombardment. (5657)
▼ Prime Minister Robert Menzies with Brigadier A. S. Allen inspects a motley-looking AIF unit during the siege. (5837)

▲ An Australian dressing station operating in a cave at Tobruk. (5628)
◀ Digging out a 1000-lb bomb from Tobruk's main square. (7535)

▲ A bren-gun post guarding the outer perimeter wire at the El Adem Road. (7470)
▼ An Australian camouflaged field gun in the desert. It was invisible from the air if no one moved. (7504)

▲ Australian troops approaching Derna. (5647/11)

▼ The death of a German tank. (7479)

▲ Australian meets Arab on a long-range patrol. (7408)

◀ Sgt W. H. Williams (second left in archway) edited, published and reported for the *Dinkum Oil*, which he produced throughout the siege. Williams's printing press was a captured Italian duplicating machine on the table in front of him. (7483)

▼ Desert patrol. (7407)

▲ Australian wounded being carried back through the barbed wire perimeter fence. (20669)

◀ Infantry tank in the streets of Tobruk. (20596)

▼ A captured Italian 149 mm field gun, one of many such guns turned against the enemy by the 'Bush Artillery'. Because of faulty ammunition, many had to be fired from a safe distance with a long rope. (20648)

Security and Prisoners

War in the desert offered many opportunities for the bold and the adventurous. The Long Range Desert Group, an irregular force which Wavell established, became past masters at adapting to the desert and using it to their advantage instead of being daunted by it. The group's principal tasks were to gather intelligence and harass the enemy and they did it successfully throughout the two-and-a-half years that the war was fought in the Western Desert.

The ability to hide in the desert became second nature to them. To the inexpert, for whom the desert was nothing but an open sand bowl, the opportunities for camouflage seemed perilously few. But in reality it was surprisingly easy to keep armoured cars, tanks and men hidden under camouflage nets or even under the ubiquitous camel-thorn, provided that everyone kept still. Enemy spotter aircraft, even at only a few hundred metres above the ground, would be unlikely to spot them — but as soon as anyone moved, they were seen immediately.

Every morning, before first light, the patrols moved out and the garrison remained behind for another day of what was frequently monotonous routine, even if they were bombarded continuously from dawn till dusk. So much had they become used to this way of living that in the end they only took notice when the bombardment stopped.

There was little to do by way of rest and recreation and the greatest luxury was to be taken, in unit transport, to a bay about 4 km to the west of the town, for a swim. It was exquisitely refreshing to be rid, if only for a few hours, of the layer of dust and grime that was an inseparable part of fighting in the desert. Within minutes of being back on the trucks heading for the units, the dust and heat and flies had taken over once again, but swimming remained one of the few real luxuries throughout the siege.

Food for both sides was little more than basic essentials. Particularly in the early part of the campaign, the Allies' diet consisted of hard biscuits, tinned cheese and bully-beef at midday; and with luck, a hot bully stew, or sausages, and a hot cup of tea at teatime. With imagination, the diet could be improved occasionally, as Headquarters Company of 2/48th Battalion demonstrated when they began fishing with home-made gelignite bombs.

The enemy were no better off. The Italians received one hot meal daily, usually stew made from tinned meat and vegetables. For the other two meals they invariably got the same rations, one tin of sardines, one ounce of honey, one bar of chocolate, half a loaf of bread, five or six cigarettes, plenty of tea and coffee and, occasionally, Italian mineral water.

The Germans fared much the same, as the diary of one captured officer reveals. 'We have now been away from Germany for two months and without butter etc. into the bargain. Our principle food is bread with something spread on it. In this heat every single bite needs a sip of water or coffee to help it down. There is no fat. If one stops to think, one realises that one drinks three times as much in Germany. Where would you find anybody in Germany who would drink water of this colour and taste? It looks like coffee and tastes horribly of sulphur.'

Among the other ranks, the German troops came to heartily dislike the fish of various indeterminate breeds, preserved in oil, which seemed to appear at every meal. On the other hand, long-lasting pressed sausage was greatly appreciated. Army bread (the Australians tried to bake it fresh every day) tended to become very hard becaue there were no tins to pack it in. And invariably there was waste and shortage of jams and honey and fruit, because the wooden boxes in which they were packed either leaked or came apart in transit.

It was thought there might still be a number of Italians at large within the perimeter, living in caves near the beach during the day and coming out at night to seek food and, possibly, information. The area within the perimeter was so large and the places to hide so numerous, that it would have been impossible to winkle out each one of them, if they were indeed there.

The Italians who were captured at Tobruk were usually described as being 'poor physical specimens' when they were taken for interrogation, and the Intelligence officers could never be quite sure whether to believe a word they said. One Italian captured, for example, insisted that two privates had recently been shot by their captain for refusing to go out on patrol. He had known the soldiers well and said both of them had been married men with families who had told their officers that fighting the English was like fighting their brothers because they had relatives in England.

The men's company was paraded, the prisoner insisted, to watch the captain shoot the men with a revolver. He missed them both. They were then dismissed, but after a warrant had been signed by their general, the captain was allowed to have another attempt. This time his aim was more accurate and he shot them both dead. It seemed an unlikely story, but desertion was a chronic problem among the enemy.

Even among the Germans desertion was occurring and among the Italians it had long been an epidemic. Between them there were so many deserters that Rommel ruled that publishing all their names would only encourage others to follow their example. After that, only the names of deserters who were sentenced to death were published. Perhaps the Italian prisoner was telling the truth.

Many of the Italians said that their officers had warned them that if they fell into the hands of the Australians, they would be killed. One ingenuously told the officer interrogating him that he was quite prepared to be shot because a soldier's life in the Italian Army had become no better than that of a slave.

The Germans had a very poor opinion of the Italians in battle and of their slovenliness behind the lines. Their officers went about so scruffily dressed, unshaven and ignored by their own men, and were so despised by the Germans that few of them even bothered to salute them.

Instructions for Allied troops when they captured enemy prisoners were simply that they were to be rapidly passed onto headquarters without examination. As soon as possible after capture, they were to be carefully searched for arms, because on several occasions Germans had surrendered only to produce concealed grenades or other weapons when they were inside the Allied lines.

Officers, NCOs and men had to be segregated and given separate escorts and all their possessions, except their paybooks and identity discs, had to be taken from them and put into an empty sandbag. Above all, no conversation was allowed between enemy officers and other ranks.

From information brought back by the few men captured by the Germans who managed to escape and make their way back inside the perimeter, it was possible to piece together a picture of what Allied prisoners of war could expect in their first weeks of captivity. An Intelligence summary warned that prisoners 'may expect and will get a rough time', but that providing they were reasonably strong, they would in time be able to adapt to their new conditions.

'The Germans will first try starvation and probably long marches,' the summary went on, 'the main object being to weaken the prisoner and break his morale. Our men must be very careful at this stage, because at the first sign of resistance or breach of discipline, the Germans will shoot to kill.'

It warned of the risk of English-speaking Germans being infiltrated among them. 'Be very careful of your next-door neighbour,' the summary cautioned. 'If he should appear to be even slightly pro-German, avoid him. Do not use violence, as it will only be visited back on you.'

The experience of those who were captured during the campaign varied very much according to where they were sent. While they were in Rommel's hands, he insisted that they were treated chivalrously and, as far as was possible in the middle of a battlefield, with care. Injured prisonery who found themselves in the hands of Italian doctors and nurses reported without exception that the standard of care and attention they were given was of the highest order within the limitations of a war situation where drugs and other medical supplies were in short supply.

For months there was a woeful lack of any sense of need for security by some of the Allies, from senior officers down to the newest private. An examination of captured Italian documents showed that a great deal of information had been obtained by the enemy simply because Allied security was so lax. 9th Australian Division Intelligence listened in on telephone conversations and found that 'matters of vital secrecy' were being discussed freely over the telephone by officers 'whose rank should preclude such obvious indiscretions.'

The Intelligence Report went on to say that, 'attempts to disguise the subject under discussion are often so rudimentary as to compel conviction that the individuals concerned simply cannot or will not understand the security limitations of the telephone. So long as there are brains at large that consider "the capital of England" to be a successful method of disguising the identity of London, so long will the efforts of the security personnel be fruitless.'

Early in May an Allied officer was arrested at 1 o'clock in the morning when he was found asking innumerable questions in the harbour about troop movements and shipping. When he was searched he was found to have a signal on him that gave precise movements of two Royal Navy destroyers, HMS *Decoy* and *Defender*. When his identity had been established, he said that all his unit knew of the destroyers' movements and he was just an inquisitive sort of person. Suspecting that anybody who wanted to know so much would probably be eager to share the information with others, he was severely reprimanded and removed from the fortress.

There were absurd lapses of security in other ways. Many of the soldiers, for example, had cameras which, until June, they were allowed to take with them into the battle area. They could then send the film back to Alexandria or Cairo for development and for months no steps were taken even to ensure that the proprietors of camera shops were not known Axis sympathisers. After June, cameras had to be left behind when proceeding to an active zone; and exposed films sent to Egypt for development and printing could only go to a few approved processors.

The news chatter came to a head when Wavell himself was approached by a woman in Cairo who asked ingenuously about the movements and plans for various units which she named. When Wavell took her to task for her indiscretion, she seemed genuinely surprised and told him that 'everyone in Cairo' was aware of the moves and that she knew her information was correct because she had heard it personally from several senior officers.

Wavell decided that, in future, loose talk — in which he included criticism of higher authority, criticism of other services and 'talk of a distinctly defeatist strain' — would be treated as being subversive of discipline and morale and therefore an offence. He gave instructions that any case of this kind in which an officer was involved was to be punished by court martial. The threat may have been effective even if the likelihood of a conviction being upheld was remote.

The Allies were not the only ones who were suffering from an inability to keep their secrets to themselves. One of the reasons which Rommel gave for not keeping the German High Command informed of his actions and why he almost never told the Italians anything, was that his experience had shown that every time he passed information to the Italians on the field or in Rome, it was common knowledge to the Allies within twenty-four hours.

The Australians were encouraged to write home frequently but after a number of gloom-laden letters had been noticed by the censors, it was decided that a word of caution from battalion commanding officers would not be out of place.

'Write home at every opportunity,' the men were therefore urged, 'but do not, before you have been in action or just afterwards, sit down and write harrowing letters home. You are a hero to your mother or wife in any case and a letter describing all the authentic details is not calculated to bring mirth and jollity into any home. Everyone knows that war is a nasty business, but why rub it in? Stress the humour and not the horror. It is hard enough for them at home without adding to their troubles.'

Mail sent back to Australia that weighed less than 4 ozs was sent free and needed no stamp. Heavier letters had to be prepaid with Australian stamps and cost one penny an ounce for each ounce over four ounces.

To save money and cut down on transmission times, a list of phrases was introduced which could be sent by simply giving a numbered code. This was then decoded at the receiving end. There was hardly an eventuality that was not covered. Number 136, for example, meant 'Hearing your voice on the wire gave me a wonderful thrill'; while 82, when decoded, was 'In bad health' and 102 meant 'Can you send me any money?'

The code allowed for subtle variations on a theme. Number 28, for instance, was a rather bland 'Fondest greetings', but 35 was a more cosy, 'Fondest love, darling' and 44 went all the way with 'Fondest love and kisses'.

Quite informative messages could be sent in this way very briefly, as in '77 / 108 / 61 / 30 / 43' which would be delivered to the frontline in Tobruk as 'Are you ill? / have not received money / you are more than ever in my thoughts at this time / keep it up / love and kisses.'

All sites had listening posts, which were manned by one or two men and were situated as close to the enemy's lines as was practicable. Their task was simply to listen and to report all they heard, and in the stillness of the desert night sound travelled with crystal clarity. Even the different sounds of coughing could be a guide to the number of men in a post.

In a captured German artillery officer's diary, a panoramic sketch had a note beside it that it had been 'drawn from cigarette lights.' The officer had been so close to the Allied lines that he could see the glow of cigarettes in some of the forward positions and so could pinpoint several of the section posts. It was an echo from World War I when the superstition started of never lighting three cigarettes from the same match. The third light gave enemy snipers time to take aim on the flame, and fire.

Humour, then as at any time, was the saviour of many a difficult situation. Just as the Italians were the butt of a thousand stories, so were the Australians back home trying to win exemption from being conscripted. Some of the stories were true, a good many were undoubtedly apocryphal. It didn't really matter and the following letter, which it was claimed that military authorities had received from a farmer asking for exemption, fell as easily into either category.

> 'I received for to go to camp, but I want to say I wont be along. I suppose they'll go me but I will put up a scrap. I ask you — is it fair? I have done two camps and lost a lot of cash. If I go to camp I get 6/- a day. If I stop home I get 15/-. At any rate whats the Army done for me? They didnt even get me made a Corporal or Lance Jack. I am a mixed farmer and its hard keeping the wolf from one door and the stork from the other and running a dairy and poultry farm. I am flat out. Another thing just between ourselves, I cant trust the wife

when I go away for a week end so how can I trust her for 90 days? I am not going to send my wife 3/- a day to spend on blokes here. I believe in home defence but in my case its home defence under the house with a shot gun. Do you blame me? Please say if leave will be granted so I will know but I'm not going away.'

The letter was reproduced in several battalion news-sheets.

As there were no recognisable roads in the whole of Libya apart from the coast road, and the escarpments were so steep and rough that they were unusable by motor transport in most places, the passes, like Halfaya between Egypt and Libya, and Sidi Rezegh on the track between El Adem and Bardia, assumed great tactical importance.

Down on the plateau, tanks and trucks could drive almost anywhere and tracks, where they existed at all, had little significance. A track was as likely as virgin desert to disintegrate suddenly into soft sand that swallowed a truck up to its axles.

After a few weeks of trying to pick out any features at all in what seemed to every novice in the desert to be an utterly barren, featureless expanse of bare sand, navigation gradually became easier. There were stunted trees and cairns; small escarpments, often only two or three metres high; and wrecked trucks, tanks and even potholes, which all gradually became useful guideposts. It certainly didn't mean that navigation became simple, or that there were any fewer of the constant arguments that raged over which stunted tree was which, and whether a rendezvous was at this sand dune, or that identical one 500 m to the west. However, with the aid of a compass and a little dead reckoning, accurate navigation did become possible.

Fighting a war in the desert has often been likened to war at sea. The armoured cars on their lonely reconnaisance, seeking out the enemy to engage, are the naval destroyers; the big guns and tank divisions are the battleships and heavy cruisers. Neither great tracts of sand nor of water have much value in themselves; they are just the board on which a deadly game is played.

As the war in the Western Desert progressed, many things changed. Equipment, weapons and particularly the men behind them improved with experience, as both sides strove constantly to remain one step ahead of their enemy. The Germans showed themselves to be much more adaptable to this new type of warfare until Montgomery arrived nearly eighteen months later. Commanders came and went with Rommel lasting longer than anyone; and the fortunes of both sides swung to and fro as the war moved swiftly from one part of the desert to another. Two things remained constant throughout the campaign — the desert itself and the endless struggle for supplies.

Everything needed to sustain men and machines in that desert had to be brought in from outside, even the wood for the latrines. Except for the old wells (and some of those had been oiled or blown up) and the occasional unpalatable camel to supplement the diet, the desert gave them nothing. Since before the Italians came into the war, Wavell had been making his preparations for a long campaign, anticipating that few supply ships would be able to get through.

He established huge bases in Egypt and elsewhere, designed to allow his troops to survive a long campaign, and he had plans for creating a base that would be large enough to serve fifteen divisions or 300,000 men.

The British built airfields and ports, roads and railways, workshops and dumps, and dug a number of new wells. If it hadn't been for these dumps, the 7th Armoured Division, headquartered near Mersa Matruh, would not even have been able to fight right up to the Libyan border when it was called in to do so.

For the ordinary soldier, standing-to in his dug-out or frontier post, taking no part in the planning process and being told as little as possible by his officers, fighting in the desert was a lonely life. Things that most men had taken for granted all their lives, like drinkable water, freedom from food rationing, letters home being unopened and uncensored, shops, pubs, trees, green grass, paddocks and cars — all these became luxuries to be dreamed of nostalgically as they waited in the immensity of the desert.

They came to hate the flies, the *khamsin*, the heat, the desert sores, the 'gyppo' tummy and the solitude. There wasn't a soldier who served there who didn't echo the feelings of the barrack-room poet who left this ungrateful ode behind when he was evacuated from Tobruk:

Land of heat and sweaty socks,
Fleas and flies and sand and rocks;
Streets of sorrow, streets of shame,
Streets for which we have no name.

Thieving, pestering, bloody wogs,
Smell of dust and stinking dogs;
Blistering heat and aching feet,
Gyppo guts and camel's meat.

Clouds of choking dust that blind,
Driving a man out of his mind;
The Arab's heaven, the Aussie's hell,
Land of bastards, fare thee well!

Lice were a constant problem and an unpleasant complication, both for the men who had to endure them and for the medical orderlies who had to try to combat them. In an order from their Commanding Officer, the 2/24th Battalion were told pointedly that some of them were 'infested with lice'. He went on, 'de-lousing is comparatively easy, but if too many men become infested, the volume of work will be beyond local resources.' The order was for all louse-ridden men to share their problem with their medical officers forthwith.

Throughout the desert campaign, one of the bogies that haunted many men was of German parachutists landing in their midst. It was known that they had been used against the Dutch with devastating effect and the very idea of the enemy falling out of the sky with bayonets already fixed was intimidating. It was this same picture, conjured up about Japanese parachutists, which would be largely responsible for the mass flight of many servicemen in Darwin nine months later.

The men inside Tobruk were told that not all the parachutists they spotted would be what they appeared to be. 'Sometimes dummy figures, often containing bombs, are dropped by parachute to deceive the enemy as to the point of attack,' an Intelligence summary warned. 'One of the first objects of parachute troops on arrival is likely to be to indicate their presence to German aircraft and to report that the terrain is suitable for the landing of troop-carrying aircraft.' There was one simple solution. 'The more parachutists who fail in the job and the greater the number who are killed, the less likelihood will there be of further landings'.

German 'tricks', like dropping dummy parachutists, were zealously blown-up by the propagandists. And what seem today to have been rather gallant gestures of defiance by the Germans, were made to look like acts of most un-British bad sportsmanship.

Under the heading, 'Irregular enemy methods of Warfare', 9th Australian Division Intelligence officers warned patronisingly, 'The Germans do not admit that there are any rules of warfare. Any form of trickery, cunning or treachery must be expected.' This followed an incident near the Belgassem *wadi* when a machine gun post had been overrun by a patrol of the 2/43rd Battalion. Three Germans had been killed and two surrendered. As soon as they came within range of their captors, however, these two suddenly drew weapons which they had concealed under their uniforms and before they were mown down by a hail of bullets, managed to wound an Australian in the stomach.

What separated this campaign from any other theatre in the war was that, in spite of the best the propagandists could do, there was a strange fellowship which bound men together, no matter what side they fought on, even while the reality of war drove them apart. The battle was fought most bitterly, yet there were few who served there who would not understand what the former commander of a Panzer troop meant when he said, years later, 'If veterans of the African campaign happen to meet, whether they are English or Australian, German or Italian, they greet each other as old comrades'.

Many Allied prisoners-of-war encountered Rommel before they were driven away to captivity. He would invariably and courteously wish them luck, often adding that they could be proud of the way they and their unit had fought. In his papers, Rommel made it clear that he believed the Australians and New Zealanders were the best infantry he had ever encountered, tough, determined and intelligent in battle. They in turn thought he was a fine and decent commander.

Perhaps, in part, it was the growing awareness of the atrocities of the SS in Europe, who were conspicuously low-key at Rommel's insistence, although they were never absent, which made the Germans in North Africa seem like a civilised enemy. You killed him, of course, because that was your job; but you didn't hate him.

One of the problems that commanders on both sides faced was that it was difficult for many junior officers and NCOs to understand that positional warfare (where troops were placed in position and for the most part stayed there, as opposed to being mobile on the battlefield or out on patrol) was not all shooting and excitement. Boredom was one of the most dangerous enemies to be overcome.

In fact it was estimated that sixty per cent of positional warfare involved working as sappers, digging in and building defences around yourself; thirty per cent was spent looking over the top of those defences and waiting for the enemy to do something; and only ten per cent of the time was actually spent shooting.

In the desert there were other problems as well. The Germans, for example, had a policy of working and moving their positions by night and then resting up during the day; the almost total lack of cover made this unavoidable. But the heat was so intense during the day, that sleep then was often impossible. In consequence, the men were always tired and operating at less than their normal efficiency.

Even personal cleanliness became a task of the first magnitude and a tedious daily chore — 'a melancholy chapter', as one German officer noted in his diary. As it was impossible to leave the positions between dawn and last light and the ground was usually hard rock just under the sand, it required a high degree of toilet-training.

In the dug-outs especially, chlorine of lime was generously used, but plagues of flies still descended on them and there was the constant danger of infection. 'The desert will not prove large enough for everyone to retire with (or without) a spade to a spot he has chosen for himself,' newly arrived German infantry were told. Behind the front line, latrines had to be constructed, but as every metre of wood had to be brought in, they were crude constructions.

Training went on constantly. The Allies were told how to recognise German and Italian units from men's uniforms and where to look for the telltale unit numbers on trucks, usually only superficially covered up when they were at the front.

They learned that German Army units could be identified by the colour of the narrow edging around the shoulder straps; and their service arm by the colour of the centre of the collar patch. White, for example, was infantry, orange the cavalry, dark blue the medical units and pink the Tank Corps.

Unit numbers on the shoulder strap were usually removed, but they learned, too, how to read an enemy identity disc. Roman and Arabic numbers had a special significance. For example, 'I/II R.16' meant that a man came from the 2nd Battalion of the 16th Infantry Regiment; whereas '2/I R.16' indicated the 2nd Company of the same regiment.

The similarity in some uniforms was always confusing. Just as the Allies in Crete wrongly believed for a while that the enemy was wearing New Zealand uniforms, so in the desert there was easy confusion, especially in the heat of battle, between the uniform worn by the German Armoured Corps and the Allied field dress. The confusion was most likely to come about when the Germans had been driven out of disabled tanks and were either waiting to be picked up, or were wandering round the battlefield searching for cover. They seldom wore helmets.

They learned how to recognise their own flares among all the colours that were bursting over the desert when fighting was at its fiercest. The Germans and Italians were issued with a variety of signalling devices that included violet and blue parachute flares and smoke cartridges, red, white and green star cartridges, and a type of Very light known as the whistling cartridge. It burned with a bright white light and gave out a shrill whistling noise that was eerie in the silence of a lull in the battle. The cartridge was about the size of a shaving stick and was made of aluminium.

Most units changed the meaning of their flare signals each month, and more frequently if they needed secrecy for an operation. Others seldom varied them, like the 5th Light Armoured Division for whom a white flare signalled, 'We are here', red that the enemy was attacking and green that enemy tanks had been spotted.

Aircraft identification signals used by both sides in the desert changed regularly. German and Italian aircraft operating at night in the battle zone carried two recognition lights, one in the front and one at the rear. Their colour varied from week to week.

Allied aircraft called on ground troops to identify themselves by firing a two-star coloured cartridge from a height of not more than 200 m. If the troops on the ground were on the move in motor transport, they had to immediately throw out a smoke generator to windward. Troops in fixed positions, such as a unit headquarters, had special signals which were changed frequently to prevent them being used by the enemy.

Both sides used some ingenious and unpleasant weapons. The Germans had a large aerial incendiary bomb, called a 250 FLAM, which contained about 65 l of highly inflammable liquid and a bursting charge of 1 kg of TNT. Much like napalm, it exploded and scattered the burning liquid over a radius of about 20 m.

And the Italians used a magnetic mine which had a photoelectric cell with an 'eye' that projected above the ground. When a shadow was cast over the eye, it made a platinum needle jerk, which in turn triggered a detonator and exploded the mine.

It needed a sudden change to trigger it and the reason why (at least in theory, because many unscheduled detonations were reported) it didn't explode at night was that the change from light to darkness was gradual. On the other hand, experiments at trying to deceive it were unsuccessful. If a piece of white paper, for instance, was put over the eye at night, the mine still exploded.

Both sides used flame-throwers, always something of an embarrassment to admit to when the war is over. They were such horrific weapons that whenever they were used by one's own side the fact was usually glossed over.

They came in two main versions. There were the flame-throwing tanks which had the nightmarish appearance of monsters belching out fire; and there were the personal, handy-pack flame-throwers carried by individuals. Typically the operator, dressed in asbestos protective clothing, carried two cylinders on his back. One held the fuel, often diesoline, the other the propellant which was compressed nitrogen, or some other gas.

They were ignited electrically and the flame on these small flame-throwers could be thrown for about 20 m although the extreme heat could be felt for 10 m beyond that. At 20 m, the flame had a diameter of about 10 m and it burnt for thirty seconds. They were normally fired in bursts so that the flame appeared to be almost constant and both range and accuracy depended in large part on the strength and direction of the wind.

If you were at the receiving end of the fire, the only defence was to take cover and let it go over your head which, it you had time, you protected with asbestos sheets which were standard issue. The man firing the thing, usually held against the thighs like a mobster wielding a sub-machine-gun, was a sitting target. Every weapon in sight would be turned on him, and a direct hit on his tanks would turn him into a human torch. If his natural inclination was then to run, his asbestos armour was likely to trip him up; and if he was captured, he could expect a rough reception from his captors. For this reason, the operators of portable flame-throwers were often protected by tanks which could pluck them to safety as soon as they ran out of fuel or were injured.

As everywhere else, both sides anticipated the use of gas by the enemy and had gas squads trained to deal with it. Anti-gas 'pathways' were issued which consisted of 50 m rolls of impregnated paper that were supposed to help troops walk out of a contaminated area. Apparatus for identifying the particular gas being used, so that the right antidote could be given, if one existed, was also available. The Germans, half-way through the desert campaign, issued protective ear-plugs for those of their men with perforated ear-drums, who would have been particularly vulnerable to gas attack. Both sides went to great lengths in any instructions that were given about gas to reinforce the idea that talk of it was purely defensive; but both sides had the means to retaliate immediately.

Meanwhile, in the lull after Rommel's first abortive attempt to crush the Australian and British defenders inside Tobruk, work went on frantically to strengthen defences, step-up the offensive patrols that were a key part of Wavell's instructions to the garrison, and generally prepare troops, exhilarated by victory, for the next round of the battle which no one doubted would be still fiercer than the last.

Holding Out

For the men defending the southern perimeter especially, the fighting and the repulse of Rommel's attack had been frightening and exhilarating. Now, for a few days, the battlefield went quiet — or at least relatively quiet by comparison with the bedlam of the previous days. Enemy tanks and infantry were still outside the wire, mostly in front of 2/48th Battalion, still pounding away at anything that moved. And small arms fire, mortars and dive-bombers continued to harass the garrison. But that had become the norm and the troops were more aware of a sudden lull in the bombardment and of a few minutes' silence, than of the enemy fire itself.

By 20 April, Intelligence reports suggested that another attack was imminent and General Morshead ordered 2/12th Battalion to prepare for an immediate pre-emptive counter-attack from its position in reserve on the western flank of the perimeter. The attack would be supported by tanks and bren gun carriers.

The operation was cancelled, however, almost as quickly as it was conceived when it was realised that the tanks and carriers would have to leave the perimeter through narrow gaps in the wire and then cross two minefields, while all the time they were exposed to near point-blank shelling.

The lull in the fighting was used by both sides to lick their wounds and prepare their next moves. Inside the perimeter work was stepped up on completing a second line of defence, the Blue Line, in case the defenders were forced back from the Red Line on the outer perimeter. At the same time, engineers placed explosives at every drinking water well and fuel dump so that they could be blown up to deny them to the enemy.

It was clear from interrogation of prisoners and from captured diaries that enemy morale was very low, and particularly gratifying to Morshead was that this seemed to be as true of the Germans as the Italians.

From his papers, it is clear that Rommel believed that the first attempt to storm Tobruk failed mainly because his divisions had not yet mastered the need to concentrate their strength at a single point in the perimeter. They could then have forced a breakthrough, secured their flanks against counter-attack and before the enemy had time to react, pushed ahead with all possible speed until they came out behind his rear.

To the extent that these were the tactics that he did use when he finally overcame Tobruk a year later (when the Australians had gone) he was right; but the cardinal error in that first attack was his own. He failed to estimate correctly the strength and resolve of the force that was holding the fortress; and inexcusably he attacked without proper intelligence.

Wavell had made it clear to Morshead that the entire defence of Egypt rested largely on his shoulders and on his ability to hold the enemy at bay at Tobruk, and they were not just empty words. Rommel, with his line of supply guaranteed and with no interference from a very dangerous enemy that at present refused to let him pass, could have pushed on into Egypt with impunity. But Wavell's injunction would have been a formidable challenge for any commander to have to shoulder. It was certainly a much greater responsibility than a divisional commander would normally be expected to carry, and particularly carry alone. For there was no one to whom Morshead could take his problems, in the way that a divisional commander in the field could normally take his problems to his Corps or even his Army Commander. His isolation meant that he was entirely on his own.

To his brigade and artillery commanders he had at all times to appear to be in complete control of every situation, and he was certainly not the kind of man to shirk from this responsibility. He was fortunate to have very able commanders immediately under him and a Chief Staff Officer, Colonel C. E. M. Lloyd, who always seemed to be at his best when the going was hardest. Lloyd was a blunt and intelligent professional soldier, but a friendly man who diligently performed his task of freeing his general of all unnecessary paperwork and detail.

He was also refreshingly practical in a way that didn't always appeal to some of the more conventional senior British officers. He wrote in his report on the constant and critical lack of signals supplies. 'We arrived with a (signals) detachment possessing three W/T sets, six telephones, three fullerphones [which were much more secure than open telephone lines which could be easily intercepted], two switchboards and one mile of cable. These stores,' he concluded cheerfully, 'were obtained mainly by theft.'

The four infantry Brigade Commanders had very different personalities which meant almost inevitably that one of them was likely to rub him up the wrong way. And so it was.

The senior of the four and the man whose advice Morshead most trusted, was Brigadier George Wootten, commander of the 18th Brigade. Wootten was a veteran of World War I — as were all four infantry commanders — and he had fought at Gallipoli and then stayed in the army after the Armistice. He remained there for only five years, however, before leaving to study law.

He qualified and then practised as a solicitor, but returned to active service as soon as the 2nd AIF was formed. If he had become, in the intervening years, a good deal too large round the middle for the Army's liking, he had lost none of the skills of a soldier that he had shown before. He had been in command of the operation to capture Giarabub, the last Allied victory before the retreat from El Agheila began.

Brigadier R. W. Tovell was probably the most congenial of the four brigadiers. Some said he lacked that streak of ruthlessness that an officer needs to take him to the most senior command, but he commanded the 2/48th Battalion, which received the full impact of Rommel's attack on Tobruk, with bravery and inspiration. He had been an accountant between the wars, but his skills as a tactician were honed as sharp as they had been twenty years earlier. He was well liked by his men.

No less popular was Brigadier A. H. L. Godfrey, commanding the 24th Brigade. He had been a more active peacetime soldier than the others and in the desert he quickly earned a reputation for leading from the front, one of the surest ways for an officer to earn his men's respect.

Brigadier J. J. Murray, the Commander of the 20th Brigade, was the fourth infantry brigadier and perhaps the one who was least compatible with Morshead. He was very popular with his men, though, to whom he was unswervingly loyal, and he was constantly taking new ideas for the conduct of the siege to Morshead. Unfortunately this was the cause of most of the friction because Morshead thought that many of the ideas were quite unworkable and Murray irritated him; but the 20th Brigade remained a brave and very effective unit.

Morshead was also well served by his two senior artillery brigadiers, J. N. Slater, who was responsible for the anti-aircraft defences, and L. F. Thompson, who was commander of the field and anti-tank guns. The role of the artillery during the siege and the counter-attacks was so critical that some commentators have argued that it was in reality primarily an artillery victory. Diplomatically Morshead was always quick to respond that neither arm could have succeeded without the other.

More than half of Slater's anti-aircraft guns had been won from the Italians, but they proved to be a great deal more reliable and safe than some of the alarming weapons that were being used by the Bush Artillery, the volunteers who turned an assortment of captured artillery pieces into a valuable asset — many of them so dangerous though that no one could stand near them when they were being fired. Slater's and Thompson's example drove their gunners on, but it was the disposition of their guns, located with intuitive skill, which was brilliant.

On the evening before the final withdrawal into Tobruk, Morshead had told his brigadiers, 'There'll be no Dunkirk here. We shall fight our way out and there will be no surrender and no retreat.' They were brave words, even if there had been nothing in the previous conduct of the troops now under his command to think they might be able to put it into practice. As they amply demonstrated, though, each one of his brigadiers was able to fire his men with a determination to achieve the impossible. Even when the troops were so weary that they scarcely knew what they were doing or where to put their feet, this belief that they could win, no matter what the odds, seldom deserted them.

And the odds *were* formidable. Against the Panzers, the brave and skilful Italian artillery, the disciplined German infantry and the undisciplined, but numerous, Italian infantry, Morshead began the siege with 35,700 men. More than 11,000 of these, however, were not front-line troops and in the base area there were nearly 6000 non-combatant servicemen, a clutter of 2800 prisoners of war and 3000 Libyan refugees who had been vaguely organised into labour battalions. One of Morshead's first tasks was to get rid of as many as possible of these useless mouths by shipping them out of Tobruk.

Of the 24,000 fighting men in Tobruk, more than 14,000 were Australian and all but a handful of the rest were British. In no other theatre of war did the British and the Australians share such respect for one another, when fighting side by side, as they did at Tobruk. The majority of the Australians were infantrymen while most of the British were artillerymen, engineers and pioneers, or came from armoured units. Each, therefore, needed the other and each lived up superbly to that responsibility.

The policy that Morshead adopted, which had come down to him from Wavell through Lavarack, was very aggressive. Paramount was that no ground was to be yielded and the defence made as deep as possible with maximum reserves held back from the perimeter for counter-attack; but there was also to be frequent counter-attack and the use of strong fighting patrols to dominate no-man's land.

Every night, therefore, patrols went out through the wire, seeking information, bringing back prisoners for interrogation, destroying or impounding whatever they found belonging to the enemy. Morshead himself moved constantly around the fortress until he became a familiar figure, not often praising and frequently criticising, but a commander the men could identify with. He was not at all popular in the first weeks of the siege, but respect for him eventually grew to very deep affection.

At the perimeter posts, he ordered new weapon pits to be constructed, insisting that the Italian pits were excellent for Italians who let a few men face the enemy while the majority sheltered underground, but that this was not how he intended to fight his battles.

After the Easter attack, engineers had laid a new minefield in the wire itself as well as in the gaps where the enemy had broken through. Many of the old mines had failed to go off and Morshead had these converted to hair-trigger detonation which was a much more reliable device.

He made other, more prosaic, demands as well. Periscopes, for example, were urgently needed, since peering over the edge of the perimeter posts to see what the enemy was doing was often fatal. The periscopes were standard equipment, but when there was a shortage of mirrors, Morshead requisitioned every mirror in the garrison except a few which he conceded the men needed for shaving.

That Rommel would strike again soon, nobody doubted: the problem that faced Morshead was trying to pin down the most likely date, when he had no aircraft for anything but the closest reconnaissance and no facilities at all for photographic reconnaissance, in spite of almost daily requests. He could not even learn much from ground reconnaissance when the ground was so flat and visibility so often reduced to near-zero by the desert sandstorms. A steady intake of prisoners was brought in on most days, but very few were of senior enough rank to have worthwhile information.

He needed to make an educated guess because it was too stressful on his men to have them constantly standing to arms on the chance that an attack was imminent. But in spite of their first rebuff, he knew that the enemy must be very confident. On the other side of the Mediterranean, the Germans seemed to be invincible. In Greece the British and Greek resistance had crumbled and the British Expeditionary Force, including the cream of the Australian troops in the Middle East who were so sorely needed now in Tobruk, had been forced to make a rapid and ignominious retreat, leaving behind all their heavy equipment.

Nearer to hand, Rommel occupied the Halfaya Pass on the Libyan-Egyptian border, as well as the escarpment around it, which prevented any reinforcements being sent to Morshead's aid from Egypt.

There were a number of false alarms when Intelligence reported to Morshead imminent attacks which never materialised. They were at least valuable as dress rehearsals. There were also genuine alarms when groups of Italian infantry were seen approaching the perimeter wire, only to find they wanted to surrender in droves of anything up to 100 or more as soon as one of them was killed or there was any show of violence.

In a typical incident, three bren-gun carriers out on patrol in the desert discovered an enemy infantry battalion approaching Tobruk from Acroma, south-west of the fortress. They raced back to alert the posts on the perimeter and were in time to warn another patrol that was heading straight into trouble.

As the enemy, who were quickly identified as Italians, deployed for attack, twelve German tanks appeared behind them. The defending artillery at once opened fire in force and with very accurate aim. Immediately, before even being called on to surrender, many of the Italians dropped their equipment on the ground and began running towards Tobruk and captivity. So disgusted were the Germans in the tanks, who were now on the Italians' flank and firing at the perimeter, that four of them deliberately turned their guns away from the Australians and British and fired a few rounds at the fast departing backs of the Italians.

That day the 2/48th took 803 prisoners. Few of these had any idea what the objective of their attack had been and they all just wanted to be out of the war in a nice safe prison camp. A senior officer was delighted to help translate a leaflet that was to be dropped over the Italian lines urging the rest of them to surrender.

The cowardice and uselessness of the Italians as infantry was a great booster to the Allied morale, reinforcing the growing conviction which most men had acquired since the defeat of Rommel's attack, that they could withstand anything that the enemy chose to throw at them.

Sometimes, of course, there was fierce fighting with the Italians and one of the bloodiest little skirmishes took place on 24 April between Italian infantry and the defending field- and machine-guns. When an enemy battalion appeared in front of the wire between S1 and S3, it was greeted with a violent burst of machine-gun fire and a barrage from the artillery. Within twenty minutes the familiar white flags were fluttering, but in that time forty of the Italians were killed.

The Italians were not the only butt for the very basic sense of humour of the besieged men. They got a few laughs from the antics of their own men as, for example, when an NCO from 2/48th went out on patrol one night and went to ground to keep a listening watch just inside an Allied minefield.

He listened for some time, separating the noises of the desert and those coming from his own lines from the enemy's, and suddenly was aware of a party of Germans talking softly, but very close to him. He kept very still but couldn't make out anything they were saying. However, being very conscientious, he kept looking ahead and straining his ears. At last the voices disappeared and he turned to make his way back to report what he had heard. No one's surprise could have been greater than his when he realised that the voices had not been German, but British; and between him and the perimeter fence was now a double-apron barbed-wire fence and a three-row minefield. He had to be retrieved at dawn, to the delight of everyone else in his unit.

Other encounters in listening posts outside the wire came close to having equally fatal results. The Garrison continued to use one of the wells in no-man's land near the point where the Derna Road came into the perimeter, and an Australian in a listening post there saw the water patrol come past him and disappear into the darkness on the way to the well.

At about the time when they should have come back, he heard footsteps and called out his challenge. The reply came immediately, 'We're Aussie soldiers!'

Gradually he heard the party coming closer until they seemed to be almost encircling him and the next moment a voice shouted, 'Kamerade, surrender!'

The sentry called back furiously, 'Be fucked, surrender! You surrender!' Then he threw himself to the ground as a nearby post which had heard the exchange turned their weapons on the enemy and opened fire. Next morning they found no dead or wounded enemy, but one very healthy German who was trying to hide.

Rommel's plans for launching another attack immediately after the first one had failed, had been abandoned when the Italians, whom he had sent to make a counter-attack, had run away when they came under British artillery fire.

On one occasion, on 22 April, he had gone forward, as he frequently did, to make a personal reconnaissance of a sector where other Italian infantry were facing the Australians. As he moved forward, he thought it was suspiciously quiet — even the enemy artillery didn't seem to be firing in that direction — and it didn't take him long to find out why.

As he crept cautiously over a rise, he was greeted with the sight of hundreds of discarded helmets, all decorated with the gaudily coloured cocks' feathers that were the emblem of the Bersaglieri Regiment. Otherwise there wasn't a trace of evidence that the Italians had ever been there. To the last man they had been either captured by an Australian patrol, or had fled.

After this incident Rommel issued an order, which was promptly countermanded by the Italian High Command, that he expected the immediate execution of any Italian officer who showed cowardice in the face of the enemy.

The portion of the hill that he had wanted to capture in that abortive follow-up attack assigned to the Italians, was the hill of Ras el Medauuar. Its possession would give him a commanding position over a large area of the perimeter and, no less important, it would deprive the Allies of the only worthwhile high ground in that part of the desert. It would also allow him to bring up his tanks and infantry out of sight of the perimeter posts.

Carrier Hill, a much smaller hill than Ras el Madauuar, for it was little more than the crest of a long ridge, was valuable for precisely this reason. It was a constant worry to the Allies that Rommel's forces could gather in the dead ground behind it before an assault on the perimeter. And, unlike Ras el Madauuar, Carrier Hill (named because of a wrecked bren-gun carrier on its slope) was outside the perimeter.

It had to be constantly patrolled and, as it was in front of his sector, this was the responsibility of the 2/48th's Commanding Officer, Lt Colonel Victor Windeyer. He sent out frequent patrols to ensure that nothing was going on behind the hill and, for days, nothing was. But then familiarity almost bred a disaster.

The routine carrier patrol went out through the perimeter, carefully making its way through the minefield, and scarcely hesitated as it rounded the side of the hill. It was, after all, not even 1000 m from the nearest post. But to their horror, they found not the usual expanse of flat sand, but a large force of infantry, a battery of 75-mm guns, four tanks and at least forty other vehicles. More by luck than anything else, they were not seen and they hurried back to report their find.

Morshead immediately ordered Windeyer to send out a fighting patrol, which he would support with tanks, anti-tank guns and artillery, to capture the troops and destroy their guns. To add confusion to the attack, he would mount two other diversionary — but worthwhile — raids, one near the Derna Road to capture enemy troops who were known to be in the Sehel *wadi*, the other on the far side of the perimeter near R51 where an enemy field artillery battery in no-man's land was causing too much damage.

Windeyer, a noted lawyer in peacetime and, unusually, a New South Welshman commanding a South Australian battalion, selected his reserve company for the mission and supported it with five bren-gun carriers as well as the other backing provided by Morshead. A Lysander spotter plane would fly low over the battlefield to drown the noise of the tanks and carriers.

At 6.40 a.m., just before first light, the Company Commander, Captain W. Forbes, a former schoolteacher with a mop of red hair, moved off, leading the attack first in a carrier and later on foot. Within minutes they had been spotted and a barrage of artillery fire was brought down on them. But it was not too accurate and they all passed safely through the wire and within an hour had reached the far side of Carrier Hill. It would have been an excellent start to the exercise if it hadn't been for the tanks and carriers which went so fast that nobody else could keep up with them. The infantry lost contact.

As it happened it was not important because the enemy turned out to be Italians and 368 of them hurriedly surrendered themselves and a small arsenal of weapons and vehicles. The patrol had lost just two men dead and seven wounded. They returned triumphantly to learn that the two diversionary attacks had been equally successful if not quite so productive. Forbes was awarded the DSO.

Windeyer was one of the best battalion commanders in the siege, a man who had a lifetime's passion for soldiering behind him, in spite of the career that he had chosen. War fascinated him, yet at a glance he was a most unlikely soldier, slow speaking, thoughtful and sometimes almost vague; but he was the ideal commander to be leading the unit that carried the brunt of repeated attacks on its sector of the perimeter. His men, resentful at first that they did not have a South Australian commander, quickly came to respect him very much and few who served under him do not speak proudly years later of having done so.

He had very quickly given his men an indicator of his style of leadership at the time of the first attack on the garrison. While the attack was still in progress and the battle raged fiercely all around them, he had sent out a patrol to capture a large group of the enemy who had been taking cover in a *wadi* about a kilometre outside the wire. If his men thought his timing was curious when they were fully occupied with defending themselves, they were soon rewarded.

The officer and twenty-two men who formed the patrol reached the *wadi* and, without wasting a moment, charged the Italians they found there with bayonets fixed. As they raced towards the enemy, shouting at the tops of their voices to add to the terror of the bayonet charge, they threw grenades ahead of them. The effect was stunning and they came back triumphantly, bringing with them seventy-five prisoners.

That same evening 1000 Italians had attacked the perimeter near S7 and had actually overrun a post in the face of fierce machine-gun fire. Windeyer had immediately ordered a counter-attack and, by sunset, another 113 prisoners had been taken and 250 driven back to their own lines. A total of 250 Italians died that day and Windeyer had made his mark.

Morshead's greatest concern was the overwhelmingly stronger armoured force that Rommel could bring against him. At the end of April there were just thirty-five Infantry and Cruiser tanks in Tobruk, in various states of repair — some were unusable for anything but spares — and a few light tanks of the 3rd Hussars which were so light that they were of little use except for reconnaisance. Wavell had another squadron of Cruisers at Mersa Matruh across the Egyptian border, but that represented the total armoured defence in Egypt. In any case, Rommel occupied the Halfaya Pass so that they could not be taken overland to Tobruk. Against this, Rommel had at least 200 tanks.

There were no reinforcements on the way, except for a few Cruisers and Infantry tanks which would merely replace the existing tanks that were out of action and for which Morshead had no replacements. The irony was that, in Egypt, he had the personnel to man six full tank regiments, many of them the crews of tanks which had been disabled or abandoned during the retreat from El Agheila and Benghazi.

The most pressing need was for long-range Cruisers which could go far behind the enemy's lines yet were fast enough to run down many of the enemy tanks and then make their escape.

Wavell shared Morshead's concern at what was a most dangerous situation. In desert warfare, which was mobile warfare once the battle moved away from the fortress, it was armour that counted even more than people. In position warfare, the aim was to destroy or disable as many people as possible on the opposing side; in mobile warfare, the side that lost the most tanks and other AFVs would almost always lose the battle. The Allies never even had them to start with once they were inside the perimeter.

Wavell took his complaint to Sir John Dill, the Chief of the Imperial General Staff and, in a personal letter, asked him to intercede with Churchill on his behalf. Either Dill's persuasion or Wavell's arguments must have been convincing because Churchill acted immediately and decided that he would no longer sit back and agree to the Navy's repeated reluctance to send in any reinforcements to Tobruk.

'I resolved not to be governed any longer by the Admiralty reluctance, but to send a convoy through the Mediterranean direct to Alexandria, carrying all the tanks which Wavell needed,' he wrote.

A convoy of tanks was just on the point of sailing for the Middle East. Some of these were earmarked for Tobruk, but the convoy was to go round the Cape to avoid the dangerous gauntlet of enemy submarines and dive-bombers in the Mediterranean. It was regarded as a suicide run by the Navy but if the tanks that Wavell needed turned off at Gibraltar and got through to Alexandria, forty days would be saved.

At a conference with his Chiefs of Staff, Churchill was emotionally persuasive. 'The fate of the war in the Middle East might turn on a few hundred armoured vehicles,' he told them. 'Even if half get through, the situation would be restored.' Indeed, even if the risk was of losing the entire convoy, it was one that must be taken.

The opposition that he had expected from the Navy dissolved and the First Sea Lord, Admiral of the Fleet Sir Dudley Pound, gave his support. Churchill then wanted to send an additional two ships with the convoy, carrying a further 100 Cruiser tanks, to increase the chance of Wavell getting what he wanted, but this time it was Dill who objected. The extra tanks, he argued, were needed for the defence of Britain and to send them to North Africa would leave the country dangerously vulnerable. In the end they compromised and an additional ship, carrying sixty-seven of the latest Cruiser tanks, joined the convoy — a total of 295 tanks if they all got through. The operation was code-named 'Tiger' and the convoy was due to sail on 23 April, ensuring that Wavell would have his tanks in Egypt by the first week in May.

By the end of April another shortage, this time of aircraft, was causing Wavell and particularly Morshead, great concern. By the last week of the month, the tiny force of fighters that remained operational was further weakened when two were shot down and two damaged on one day. Against them the enemy aircraft seemed almost unlimited in number as well as being very modern and well piloted. The Italian pilots, unlike their colleagues in arms on the ground, were usually excellent and brave fighters.

The only cause for satisfaction was that a new policy of using the heavy anti-aircraft guns to put up an umbrella barrage against the enemy, instead of aiming for one plane at a time, seemed to be reducing casualties. The first time it was extensively used in a raid on the harbour, six out of thirteen enemy planes were destroyed.

By 25 April the situation was so serious that the remaining Hurricanes were ordered out of Tobruk by the RAF. It was believed that to leave them there was to invite their certain destruction, and throughout the Western Desert, there remained just thirteen Hurricanes.

Morshead complained bitterly, first to the RAF that, without fighter support, it would be impossible to use the Lysander for directing the artillery, and without the Lysander, the artillery would be weakened to the point where it would be ineffectual unless gun crews were firing over the sights; and secondly to General Beresford-Peirse, the Commander of the Western Desert Force.

To Beresford-Peirse he sent a signal that it would be disastrous for morale to see the sky empty of Allied aircraft with the enemy planes bombing, machine-gunning and dive-bombing at will. Beresford-Peirse was sympathetic, but adamant. Until he had more fighters, he could not afford to lose those he had.

Proof of just how vulnerable Tobruk would now be to attack

from the air, when she had no fighters with which to defend herself, came very soon after this exchange. Twenty-four German dive-bombers came roaring in out of the sun to attack the anti-aircraft defences near the harbour and almost at once four of the guns were put out of action and fifty of their crew were dead or injured. The gunners never even saw them coming.

The anti-aircraft gunners fought more determinedly than ever. They used the 'porcupine' formation, facing the guns outwards, and then firing continuously at more than 65° elevation, which the dive-bombers found difficult to penetrate. One of the hardest lessons some gunners failed to learn was that those who resisted the temptation to take cover when a raid was at its height, and instead kept on firing, were by far the most likely to survive.

In the last twenty days of April, the anti-aircraft guns went into action against a total of 386 dive-bombers in twenty-one separate actions. The constant strain led to a few gunners having to be taken away, victims of what the others called without malice or sympathy, 'going troppo.'

With their fighters taken away, the gunners clearly had to find some other way of protecting themselves. From overhead, they had virtually no protection at all. To build them new positions, however, would cost a lot of money and there was in any case no time. The ingenious solution was to build a series of dummy AA posts and then, if the real guns were moved frequently, the argument went, the enemy would never know which were which.

It certainly offered no guarantee against being killed, but it would halve the chance of being hit in the first place. Brigadier Slater, who was in charge of the anti-aircraft guns, appointed a camouflage officer who immediately began work constructing the dummy sites near the real guns. They were very authentic and a great deal of ingenuity and work went into their design and construction. As well as having dummy guns, they were equipped with dummy people, vehicles, tracks and dumps. There were even fireworks and smoke canisters which simulated the guns' flashes and the dust that was always created when they were fired.

At the same time, the real gun positions were strengthened and dug deeper into the ground. The combination of measures that were taken were highly successful and the enemy responded to the dummies just as Slater had hoped. The guns never experienced the same terrible casualties again, in spite of equally severe raids on the fortress.

Other dummies had been used since the earliest days in the desert and by both sides. Dummy tanks, for example, were used by Rommel and Beresford-Peirse, though more extensively by the Germans. They were built in Tripoli, (the port in Tripolitania which the Germans occupied at the western end of Libya) using cardboard and were then mounted on motor cycles with sidecars.

The purpose of them, on both sides, was to confuse the enemy as to the strength of an armoured unit as well as the likely point on the perimeter where an attack would take place. When tanks were taken out of the line for repair or after battle-damage, dummies would take their place during the night. The Germans never actually used them during an attack, taking them far behind the front line if there was any risk of them being discovered, but the Allies knew of their existence, if not their deployment, very soon and were soon using them as extensively — and as coyly — themselves.

Dummies were also used as decoys. A battalion on the left flank reported, during the hours before the Germans attacked, that thirty dummy soldiers, wearing uniforms filled with straw, had appeared near some scrubby bushes only a short distance from the perimeter fence. There didn't seem any reason for them to be there and, on closer inspection through binoculars when the sandstorm had died down, it could be seen that they were not so much dummies as objects of some kind dangling from a strand of wire. There was no sign of any enemy anywhere near.

Next morning a patrol went out, the company commander no longer able to contain his curiosity. The patrol went cautiously and they were within 20 m of the curious dummy-like creatures when forty enemy suddenly appeared from concealed positions all around them. It was the simplest of ambushes. The dummies never had any purpose except to lure the defenders out so that prisoners could be taken for interrogation.

Compared with his troubles with the Air Force, Morshead was well served by the Navy and particularly by the Naval Officer in charge, Tobruk, Captain F. M. Smith who had turned down a bigger and better ship so that he could remain in Tobruk. Smith had a fleet of waifs and strays, from gun-boats and whalers to yachts and trawlers. Their primary purpose was the dangerous carriage of supplies between Britain and Tobruk, literally keeping the fortress alive.

The Naval Inshore Squadron was the official name of the unit that did this dangerous task, but it also had sharp teeth. It bombarded the town of Bardia so fiercely that its inhabitants were forced to flee; and then it went round the corner and did the same to Salum where the occupying troops were also largely withdrawn.

Meanwhile, back in the perimeter, the force busied itself preparing for the next attack which nobody had any doubts would take place soon. As with Morshead, the only question occupying their minds was when Rommel would decide that the moment was right.

Under Siege

While Churchill and his War Cabinet were urging Wavell and Morshead to hold up the Germans at any cost and to resist until the last man fell, Rommel was receiving rather more conflicting orders from his own High Command.

Tobruk must be reduced at the earliest opportunity, he was told, and with that he could be entirely sympathetic. But he had been told first to make no move in this direction until his reinforcements (mainly the 15th Armoured Division) arrived, and then to make the attack with the Italians he had available.

But Rommel had learnt from the first attack that it would be folly to risk another attack against an enemy that would be even stronger than the demoralised force he had expected to find the first time, without the necessary strength behind him. And strength meant armour.

The Germans had suffered a serious blow only two weeks before when an Italian convoy of five merchant ships, escorted by three destroyers, was intercepted in the Mediterranean as it was bound for the Middle East. The entire convoy, including the destroyers, was sunk and among the cargo that went to the bottom were transport and heavy equipment (including tanks) for the long-awaited 15th Armoured Division.

Further delays in building up the Axis strength were becoming unacceptable and Rommel had to act. Hitler suggested sending more Italian infantry instead of tanks but Rommel, who had seen enough of Italian infantry to last him the war, scoffed at the idea and replied that it would be a waste of valuable troop-carriers to use them for Italians.

By the end of April, however, he knew that he had to act or face a counter-attack from Morshead which might be too strong for him to resist, even with the armour that he had. He therefore gave orders for the preparation of a full-scale attack using all his formations and striking simultaneously along the whole front. Knowing that anything he told the Italians would be available to the British within twenty-four hours, Rommel was necessarily cautious about the detail that he passed to them and it did not include any dates or times, nor the place in the perimeter where the main bridgehead would be made.

The information that he sent to Berlin, however, was enough for the German High Command to send immediately to Libya one of its most senior officers. General von Paulus was senior to Rommel in age and experience and he had been, until recently, Chief of Staff of the 6th German Army in Western Europe. He arrived in Tobruk on 27 April to find Rommel on the point of launching his attack.

Paulus's brief was to insist that Rommel obey orders when he received them (and that meant delaying the attack) and to permit Rommel to do nothing until he, Paulus, had carried out his own reconnaissance and held discussions with Rommel's senior officers. In spite of this, Paulus had changed his mind within forty-eight hours and was agreeing with Rommel that the attack should take place as soon as possible. The advantage of striking fast was that every day that slipped by made Morshead and Tobruk that much more dangerous and difficult to defeat. And his Intelligence reports told him that a large convoy loaded with armoured vehicles was on its way to the Middle East (though not the much more important information that it was to be diverted at Gibraltar).

On 27 and 28 April, the defenders inside the perimeter fence noticed that the number and the strength of enemy air raids was increasing. In one attack, Naval Headquarters was almost destroyed; and large numbers of vehicles could be seen moving up nearer to the fence and then across towards the Acroma Road from where all the previous attacks on the western sector had arrived.

The Blue Line was now almost complete with the laying of tactical minefields, and much of the work that had been ordered for improving the perimeter posts was taking effect.

On the 29th, the air attack became even more intense and there was constant dive-bombing and machine-gunning of the forward posts and reserve battalions and, as always, the artillery. In one attack alone, three men of the 2/10th Battalion were killed and eight wounded. They had all been guarding Morshead's Headquarters at Fort Pilastrino.

Then, at lunch time, a solitary enemy aircraft came low over the 2/24th sector and attacked an old stone hut, covered with a tarpaulin roof, where a company commander was conferring with several other officers. One was killed and four, including the Company Commander, were seriously wounded.

At two o'clock three more men died when their gun positions at the junction of the El Adem and Bardia roads were attacked. Again they had no protection from the air. Then, at four o'clock the harbour was heavily raided and the ship *Chakla*, which only that morning had brought in a battalion from Mersa Matruh, was sunk. It prompted an order that, from then on, troops were only to be moved by ship after dark.

The new battalion, which had come to reinforce the Garrison, was the 2/32nd, part of the 25th Brigade. It was only sent at the last minute because the battalion which should have gone, the 2/25th, had not yet arrived in Palestine from Australia. The 2/25th was part of the 24th Brigade, which was already in the perimeter, but Wavell decided that the situation was too dangerous to risk waiting until it arrived when it still had to be kitted out and given basic desert training.

Even this battalion arrived short of a company, which had not embarked on the *Chakla* when a big storm blew up. She sailed with the men who were already on board and reached Tobruk safely at 8 a.m.

There was no respite on the 29th so long as daylight lasted, but, with darkness, the intensity of the firing died away. There was the usual last artillery bombardment as both sides did their evening ranging and then the enemies, separated by only a few hundred metres of sand, settled down to a night of comparative calm, punctuated only by the occasional burst of fire as one or other trigger-happy post manned by the Italians, fired at a shadow in the dark.

Three lighters slipped into Tobruk harbour during the night, unloaded six Infantry tanks and then moved noiselessly out into the

Mediterranean, taking with them German tanks captured in the Easter battle, for examination by experts in Britain.

The 2/48th Battalion, which had borne the brunt of the enemy's attacks along its 20-km front, was well overdue for a rest. It had lost fifteen of its men killed and another twenty had been injured; but in return it had killed many of the enemy and taken 1375 prisoners and a great deal of equipment.

Relief was to be provided by the 2/24th Battalion, which had been in reserve. The changeover took place without incident and with as little unusual noise as possible which might have alerted the enemy to the fact that, for a time, the sector was in the hands of relatively inexperienced men. As the 2/48th moved back to take over the defence of the Blue Line, it was the first time since it had left Benghazi that other troops had stood between it and the enemy. It was a pleasant sensation. The commander of the new front-line battalion was a twice-decorated veteran of World War I, Lt Colonel Allen Spowers, who was to be as effective in his own way as Windeyer. He was a strict disciplinarian, a good tactician and his visible bravery was a constant inspiration to his officers and men.

Spowers immediately put his men to work deepening trenches and strengthening the sangars. He ordered every available sandbag to be filled with rubble and then put into position as fire-steps in the posts, so that each position's fire power could be increased.

As the first tinges of dawn touched the horizon on the last day of April, clouds of dust away to the west in the direction of Acroma indicated that the enemy was already on the move in force. From higher up, on the slopes of Ras el Medauuar, Major Fell, who was commanding that dangerous sector of the perimeter, studied the activity through binoculars and estimated that there were at least 100 vehicles, though it was impossible to see how many were AFVs and how many troop-carrying trucks.

Further north, another movement caught his eye and he saw twenty more vehicles moving toward the perimeter along the escarpment. This time there was no doubt that they were all armoured. Constant observation was impossible because already the dust was rising as an early *khamsin* came through and there were only frustrating glimpses of the enemy through chinks in the wall of sand that hid them from view. The spotter aircraft went up and was able to confirm Fell's assessment and then help the artillery to range on the convoy, which immediately broke up when it was fired on.

By nine o'clock the observers on the slopes of the hill could see infantry as well and, in a brief lull in the *khamsin*, they watched through glasses as the troops, who appeared to be German, got out of the trucks that had brought them from the direction of Acroma. They began to advance in line, stopping at a point just out of range of the British artillery, approximately 4000 m from the wire, where they sat down.

Fell asked the artillery to lob a few shells in their direction, even though the forward observer had advised that they were not in range and the gunners, reluctant to use their precious ammunition, had at first objected and then lobbed a few shells across the desert at extreme range to make their point. They fell harmlessly in the sand well short of their target.

Shortly afterwards, the dust came up more thickly than ever, and for the rest of the day there were only the occasional tantalising glimpses of enemy activity. Each time, however, they seemed to be closer and the infantry could now be seen to be both German and Italian. All the indications were that another attack on Medauuar was imminent, although there was no hard proof. Even the pigeons which the Italians used for carrying messages (their military pigeons were ringed and marked with the letter 'M' followed by a serial number) were safely out of range of the Australian sharp-shooters.

Apart from superficial facelifts to the old Italian perimeter posts and strengthening of the exposed sangars, which left them just as vulnerable as before to the guns of the tanks, little had been done, or indeed could be done, to improve the defences. This was particularly worrying with the anti-tank defences, when there was clearly every likelihood that the first assault would come from the German armoured units.

Most of the relatively sophisticated anti-tank weapons that came later in the war were not available then and the field artillery, which ideally should have fired over its sights at minimum range if it was to be used effectively against tanks, was too far back. In the whole of Spower's 6-km sector, with its twenty-three perimeter posts, there were only eight static and two mobile anti-tank guns, all extremely vulnerable even to a small infantry assault.

The best that could be achieved, which Colonel Lloyd, Morshead's Chief of Staff, put into effect immediately, was to bring forward the tanks of the 3rd Armoured Brigade and position them, with another anti-tank company, behind the Ras el Medauuar sector and about 1000 m behind Spowers's headquarters. In this position they were on the track that led to the Pilastrino Ridge above which Morshead had his own headquarters and where most of the field guns were located.

The morning and afternoon passed without any major incident and with neither side able to see the other through the blinding, choking duststorm. Just keeping weapons and vehicles clean was a full-time job and the sand got into every tiny opening in clothing and body. The fear that the enemy might make their assault during one of these storms, which had been cause for much concern in the first days in the fortress, was now hardly considered. Communication would be impossible and the tanks, in particular, would certainly lose their way and stumble into either a minefield or an anti-tank position.

It was certain that they would move up their troops under cover of the dust, but Morshead was convinced that they would go no further than that. Dive-bombing attacks still occurred every day, whether the sand was blowing or not, and the cloud of dirt that was generated could rise for hundreds of metres, but more often it kept much closer to the desert floor and visibility from above, looking down, was often clearer than at ground level.

Meanwhile, a 105-mm gun, sited far outside the range of anything in the fortress, pounded away alarmingly though intermittently at Morshead's headquarters or at the harbour, whatever the weather was like. The effect of being on the receiving end of a 105-mm shell was something like being caught halfway down a railway tunnel when an express train comes in at each end.

Visibility didn't begin to improve until late in the afternoon when Spowers visited Fell in his Company Headquarters which, even as the crow flew, was about 10 km from his own headquarters. He could now see for himself some of the strength of the enemy's infantry and AFVs, which were clearly massing near the Acroma Road. It had something of the feel of a medieval battle when the two protagonists pitched their tents at each end of a long field, viewed each other warily and then waited for daylight for the battle to begin. 'Like jousting knights', a German officer described the opposing armies, both clearly visible a few sand dunes away. The simile was apt.

Captain L. G. Canty, on the right of the Battalion's sector (he had taken over command of the company whose officers had been bombed in the stone hut) reported a platoon of the enemy moving towards his position, followed by some motor cycles. The message was timed at 5 p.m. and, from that moment, the reports began to come in thick and fast.

At 5.30 the 2/23rd Battalion, whose sector included the Derna Road, was attacked by dive-bombers and one man was killed and four others wounded. At 5.45 a barrage of shells began falling right across the western sector and a lookout on Ras el Medauuar reported four vehicles and about 150 infantry advancing towards him. Then the shelling stopped, always an ominous sign.

Much of this activity was going on behind the hill, so that most of the posts had no idea what was happening. There was still no sign of any tanks, but the Medauuar lookout reported a second wave of foot soldiers, not as big as the first, but still heading straight towards him. He noticed that they were much better dispersed than on previous days, when they had tended to move in bunches that made an attractive target for the Allied artillery and machine guns. Then, at seven o'clock that evening, the first tanks came into sight, rumbling along behind the infantry.

Post R1 began to take a heavy battering from enemy artillery and mortars, but there was no clear reason why it was being singled out. The dust was so thick — from the movement of the tanks and other vehicles, not the *khamsin* — that it was impossible, even from the top of Ras el Medauuar, to count the tanks.

As the sun slipped down behind the horizon and the dust-laden sky turned to brilliant hues of gold, red and pink, four planes came out of the western sky on a course that took them directly over the garrison. Moments later came squadrons of dive-bombers, but instead of laying a pattern of bombs over the whole of the western sector, as far back as headquarters, as they had done on previous days, they dropped the lot on the south side of Ras el Medauuar. The noise was heard throughout the perimeter and for the men of 2/24th Battalion it was deafening and terrifying. The whole sky seemed to be filled with aircraft letting loose their bombs, screaming down until it seemed unavoidable that they would plough straight into the desert and then pulling back at the last second, machine-guns rattling the concrete posts and pillboxes.

The attack seemed to last for ever, like an earthquake, but as suddenly as they had come, the planes suddenly weren't there. Yet, even as men picked themselves up and wiped the sweat from their eyes, the onslaught was on again. This time thirty dive-bombers swept in on the north side of the hill and, with a great noise like a thunderclap, that seemed to last to infinity, the bombs landed.

This time one of the aircraft didn't recover from its dive. Perhaps the pilot had been hit by the anti-aircraft fire that added to the deafening noise and continued without respite until the last aircraft had disappeared from view, or perhaps he just left his recovery and climb until it was too late. Whatever the reason he piled straight into the desert to the delight of the watching Australians and British. A cheer went up to speed the pilot on his way.

As the last light went out of the day, many more infantry took advantage of the diversions caused by the air attack to move closer to the wire and they gathered about 3000 m in front of it. Spowers had ordered every man to stand to arms and to expect an immediate attack, and suddenly the enemy's artillery opened up with a barrage along the whole 4-km length of wire. The noise was indescribable and, if anything, even more frightening than the sound of the dive-bombers.

'If Jesus Christ himself had come down at that moment, none of us would have been surprised', an old member of the 2/24th recalled years later. 'It was like a bloody fanfare to herald the end of the world!'

The order that Rommel had given his commanders was simple. 'The Africa Corps will force a decision in the battle around Tobruk during the night 30 April–1 May by an attack from the west.'

Two of his German divisions were to make the first assault and they would be followed in, with considerable misgivings on Rommel's part, by two Italian divisions. By 8 p.m. they were to have attained their first objective, the penetration of the perimeter on both sides of Ras el Medauuar. Once there, they would wait until dawn the next morning when they would push on through the Allied positions, continuing their attack through Bianca and

Pilastrino, capturing Morshead's headquarters as they went, and not stopping until they had reached their final objective, the town and the harbour in Tobruk itself. Rommel was confused about the significance of Bianca which he believed was a strongly defended position as was shown on the Italian map of the fortifications that he was using. In fact there was almost nothing there.

The softening up by the dive-bombers and the artillery allowed the German engineers to make narrow penetrations in the wire, one on the left just north of S3 and the other near S7 higher up the escarpment. Other troops then went close to the fence and lifted the mines between these two posts while tanks pulled away the wire with grappling irons, or blew it in with bangalore torpedoes. The anti-tank ditch at that point was incomplete and was so shallow that it was not an effective barrier at all.

At 8.15 red and green flares soared high into the night sky and at once the artillery barrage that had been concentrated on the wire, turned with pinpoint accuracy to the posts themselves. The fire was intended to keep the defending forces' heads down while the first major penetration was made. Streams of tracer drifting in towards the wire alerted the men in S5 and S7 that an unknown number of infantry were approaching.

The tanks, which had been a part of the assault to open up the bridgehead, moved through the wire but so fierce was the fire and so dark the night that their arrival was never reported to Divisional Headquarters. In fact, so confused was the situation and so bad the communications that by the time the message reached the duty officer at Divisional Headquarters it had lost all sense of urgency. He logged the whole formidable assault with the words, 'May indicate a half-hearted attack at dusk.'

At 9 p.m., little more than an hour-and-a-half after the attack had started, a green and white Very light told Rommel that his first objective had been met and that his forces were in possession of Ras el Medauuar. The enemy bombardment gradually wound down. In fact, he was not in possession of the whole hill. His troops had occupied the old building at the top of the hill, which had been used by the Allies for artillery observation, but the perimeter posts themselves had not yet been touched.

Spowers' headquarters, which was well back from the front, was almost completely cut off and he knew little more than Morshead who was much closer than his own troops on the perimeter. He was frustrated at not being close to the action with his men, but the system of communications that existed meant that to be in contact with all his companies and posts, he had to remain at his headquarters.

Communications throughout Tobruk were as inadequate and vulnerable as they had been when the Allies first entered the fortress when they were pursuing the Italians westwards. Few of the units had received more than a fraction of the battle equipment that was laid down as being necessary, and one battalion had arrived with no means of communication except a few old flags.

In many cases they had been able to make good their shortages with equipment taken from the Italians, but they had lost it all again when they had been forced to retreat from Benghazi. They had neither the time nor the transport to bring it with them.

The only organised method of communication between headquarters and the various units was a telephone network using lines that emanated from Fortress Headquarters and more or less followed the line of command. Lines went from Headquarters to the battalions; from the battalions to the companies; and, in some cases, but far from all, from companies to their platoons. As a general rule, the only perimeter posts which had a telephone were those where the platoon commanders had their headquarters.

Between any of these points there was almost no lateral means of communication — company couldn't speak to company, nor post to post and even most of the battalions were out of touch with each other by direct line. If any of them needed to communicate, they had to ring back to Fortress Headquarters where the switchboard would connect them.

The inevitable result was, at best, a chronic shortage of lines. A system of priority calls was introduced, but there were so many of these that it was all but useless and all it achieved was to ensure that those who doubted the urgency of their call never got through at all. Any officer could ask for a priority call by franking the message 'Immediate', or just demanding a priority telephone call; but he was then answerable for his action and he could be called on at any time to prove that the situation really was urgent.

The lines themselves were always breaking or failing, even before the siege began; when the battle was on, they seldom worked at all. The lines were almost invariably laid above the ground where they could be broken by men walking on them, let alone by enemy artillery and mortar fire. But this was only because the alternatives were even less satisfactory.

If they were strung up on poles, as the Italians had done, they were constantly being shelled or used as ranging marks by the enemy artillery, to such a degree that most of the poles had been pulled down on Morshead's orders. And if they were buried, they were either moved and then lost in the constantly shifting sands, or they were destroyed as effortlessly by enemy shelling as if they lay on top of the ground.

What was more, if they were under the ground, they were very difficult to find, let alone repair — impossible by night and extremely dangerous by day. And in many areas the ground was so rocky, anyway, that there were only a few centimetres of sand on the surface.

In another, better organised situation, duplicate lines would have been laid, with alternative routes between posts or companies or direct to headquarters, but there was not enough equipment to maintain even one line in Tobruk and this was never an option.

Supplementing the line network was a wireless telegraphy network relying on coded Morse code tapped out by operators, but it was a notoriously inefficient substitute.

Cyphering and then decoding messages which were usually urgent — no commander would waste his time using Morse if the matter wasn't urgent — caused interminable delays and numerous mistakes, and if a brief message was not to take all day to send or receive, it could only be used by trained operators. In Tobruk there was the added complication that there were few facilities for recharging the batteries that the sets needed.

The only reliable means of communication throughout the siege were the independent cables and wireless networks used by the artillery to communicate with their forward observation officers and between each other as well as with brigade and Fortress Headquarters. The artillery had priority in the distribution of the best equipment and they had their own engineers for repairing any breaks in the line immediately they occurred. Only the most urgent messages, though, if they did not concern the artillery, could be passed over their lines.

Inside his underground bunker cut into the escarpment above Fort Pilastrino, Morshead heard little of the bombardment that had taken place that evening. Only when he went outside could he hear the distant rumble of bombing and the staccato rattle of the anti-aircraft guns. At 8.30 he had felt as much as heard the huge explosion as the bangalore torpedos, long metal tubes packed with explosives and lashed to a board, ripped an enormous hole in the wire near S7. At eleven o'clock he went to bed.

Colonel Spowers, in 2/24th Battalion's Headquarters, had not enjoyed any sleep. Infuriated by the lack of information coming back from the perimeter, he had been forced to cool his heels and wait. It appeared that he had no contact with any of his units in the front line. Then, at 1.15 a.m., when the battlefield sounded fairly quiet, a message reached him via the 51st Field Regiment that his forward company, commanded by Captain Canty, needed help urgently because the enemy were closing in fast on his company headquarters.

The commander of Canty's right hand platoon, Lt J. S. Rosel, who had got the message through to Spowers, had sent one of his sections to aid Canty and now Spowers ordered three bren-gun carriers to make all possible speed and go to his rescue.

The carriers set out at once, but immediately ran into heavy ground mist which had settled in the hollows, and lost their way. They retraced their steps and got back into the perimeter safely, and Spowers sent out a foot patrol instead. But this, too, got lost in the mist and was forced to return. Visibility was now down to zero, but the carrier commander volunteered to try once more: again he lost his direction, however, and had to abandon his mission. All Spowers could do now was cross his fingers and wait.

From the sketchy and unreliable information that had filtered through, Spowers believed that the enemy were probably holding their bridgehead in front of Ras el Medauuar somewhere in the sector between S3 and S7; and from fragmentary messages and rumours he thought it likely that the enemy had turned right as soon as they were inside the perimeter, and had moved down until they were somewhere in the vicinity of R5 where a track to El Adem came through the wire. Wherever they were, it seemed likely that they would hold their positions until dawn and then launch an all-out offensive whose objective would certainly be the rapid subjugation of the fortress.

When Morshead was woken at dawn on 1 May, Lloyd confirmed

that the enemy had penetrated the wire around Ras el Medauuar, but that little else was certain. Communications had remained broken all night. Morshead decided to wait until he had a better appreciation of the situation before ordering any countermeasures.

In 2/24th's Headquarters Spowers was no better informed, but there was a rumour that the enemy were digging in on the other side of Ras el Medauuar from the point where the bridgehead had been made, probably near R7. (The letters R and S to describe the posts were originated by the Italians who took the capital letters of the Italian words for right and left. 'R' meant the right-hand side of the hill when looking at it from outside the perimeter, and 'S' the left-hand side.)

Spowers sent out a section of bren-gun carriers under Lt J. T. Shelton, with orders to investigate the report and to make some kind of appraisal of the situation as a whole.

Shelton, a grazier before he volunteered, took only his own carrier, which he drove himself, and a crew of three. At 6.30 he set out and men in a nearby post watched as the carrier disappeared in the heavy mist.

He drove cautiously and occasionally small arms fire would open up on him, fired blindly into the mist. Once, near the Acroma Road, he swore that he was being shot at by his own men, but he didn't slow down to find out. Near R7 he found evidence of newly dug weapon pits, but the enemy had either abandoned them and moved on, or was hiding until he passed, for there was no sign of life. He reported back to headquarters and also made contact with Major Fell whose headquarters were at the top of Ras el Medauuar.

Occasionally the mist would clear and, from Battalion Headquarters, Spowers could see the carrier climbing the side of the hill and obviously heading towards Fell. At 6.42 Shelton's voice came weakly over the radio reporting that he had just passed a wooden hut which seemed to be full of Italians. With no fire power to tackle them he pressed on.

At 7.10 he reported that visibility was down to 200 m and that he was being fired on continuously by the enemy, but that he would still try to reach Fell. Although visibility was low with mist clinging to the hill, for much of his progress officers in Headquarters had been able to see him. But just when he was almost at the top, the mist swallowed him again and he was hidden from view. That was the last that was heard from him.

An hour later, when the sun broke through the mist, they saw the carrier again, but this time it was beside the Acroma Road, burning fiercely. Shelton had unwittingly run straight into a group of German tanks which had been standing on the south-east slope of Ras el Medauuar and they had opened fire on him before he realised what had happened.

He was killed instantly, but his foot was pressed hard on the accelerator and the carrier kept going. The man beside him leant over his body and steered the carrier back to the Acroma Road, taking advantage of the fog to elude the tanks which were still firing after him. Just as they reached the road, a chance shell hit the carrier again, this time in the petrol tank, which caught fire. The injured survivors leaped for their lives and took cover until another carrier arrived to rescue them.

Morshead's reluctance to retaliate immediately with a counter-attack was brought about by a suspicion that the whole affray round Ras el Medauuar might be nothing more than an elaborate diversion to draw out his reserves while the main assault took place somewhere else. What he needed above all was accurate information and that was conspicuously lacking.

An early report spoke of 200 tanks massing near S3, but this seemed so improbable that he insisted that it be double-checked. The second report mentioned forty tanks which seemed on probability to be much too few. He decided again to wait until he had sounder information on which to base his next move.

For the first hour after dawn, the exchange of fire was half-hearted, as though both sides were reluctant to break into that one brief part of the day when the desert was enchanting and cool. Then, as the mist lifted and the first heat of the sun touched the waiting men, the barrage began.

As the shells lobbed down, the now all too familiar howl of the sirens on the dive-bombers, designed to add to their horror, came louder and louder. Sweeping down on the forward posts and the vulnerable exposed sangars that had not already fallen during the night, the Stukas sprayed everything that moved with a deadly hail of machine-gun fire.

Another patrol, which had been sent out to reach Fell on Ras el

Medauuar after Shelton's death, was driven back by fierce enemy fire, but not before it had seen six German tanks waiting on the far side of the hill.

What had happened the night before, although nobody on the Allied side of the perimeter was aware of it, was that when the bombardment stopped at 8.30 p.m., two penetrations of the wire were made by enemy tanks, one north of Ras el Medauuar near S5, the other near R1. Once inside, the tanks had closed up to prevent grenades being lobbed through their visors, and had settled down for the night.

As the fog lifted these tanks went on the offensive, standing over the nearest positions to where they were huddled and blasting them to pieces. At 8 a.m., the watching troops saw an even more chilling sight, as about forty tanks, in line abreast, came over the skyline south of Medauuar and moved eastwards towards a sector defended by the 2/15th Battalion. Some were towing anti-tank guns.

Behind them again were yet more tanks, another line of forty moving abreast and travelling at speed, seemingly oblivious of the artillery and anti-tank fire being poured down on them from half a dozen directions.

The British gunners had at first been reluctant to fire on the tanks at all because they were so close to the Australians, but as soon as their observers were satisfied that they had the exact range, they opened up.

The brunt of the attack fell on the infantry in the front line, and on the few hapless gunners and others who were still in sangars that had not yet been subdued. With no protection at all against an enemy standing over them, they were quickly silenced or captured. Worse off still were those who found the enemy menacing them with flame-throwers.

Some, realising the hopelessness of their position, surrendered immediately; others defiantly, even recklessly, resisted to the last. A gun of the 26th Anti-Tank Regiment, for instance, which was dangerously located in open country behind Forbes' Mound, a small pimple in the desert north-east of Ras el Medauuar, opened fire on all forty tanks in the first wave as they came into sight.

Pieces of the gun were flying off in all directions as they were struck by fire from the tanks, but the gun commander kept firing until there was almost no gun left, when he fell, mortally wounded. He had stopped two of the tanks in their tracks and, perhaps confused by the violence of the attack on them, the rest ran straight on to a minefield. There seventeen of them came to an abrupt halt and for the rest of the battle they stayed there, immobile, but firing in every direction as though they were heavily armoured pillboxes. Many were destroyed and the rest extricated themselves and made a hasty retreat.

Major Fell, who was proving so hard to reach on Ras el Medauuar, could see German tanks surrounding s1 from his own headquarters in s2. From a distance of less than 200 m, the tanks were bombarding the post and shortly afterwards, the platoon commander, Lt Walker, led his men out of the pit in surrender and they were marched away.

The tanks then moved on to his own post, wiping out a couple of sangars on the way, and halting again at a distance of 200 m. They opened fire at once, sending the sandbags hurtling into the air. Riding on the back of each tank were two or three infantry whose job was to lob grenades into each weapon pit as they came within range after the initial softening-up. Like Walker, Fell knew that the only alternative to surrender was the death of everyone in the post and he, too, went out with his arms held high. As they passed through the perimeter wire, Fell saw for the first time the enormous hole that had been breached. Like great robots, three tanks led the way while two more followed to discourage any attempt to escape.

They were well treated by the Germans who seemed sure that Tobruk would fall before the day was out; and before they were marched the 25 km to Acroma, they were seen by Rommel who wished them luck. It was of these soldiers that the German leader wrote in his diary, 'Fifty or sixty Australian prisoners were marched off close behind us — immensely big and powerful men who without question represented an élite formation of the British Empire, a fact that was also evident in battle.'

After s1 and s2 had fallen, s3, R, R1, R2 and R3 were quickly captured. R4 managed to hold out until noon and then it, too, was forced to surrender. On the other side of the hill the hapless s5, which had been at the centre of the bridgehead, had been overrun at first light but s6, where Canty's predicament had caused such concern during the night, was not surrendered until 9 a.m. By then seventeen of the twenty-six men in the post were casualties. S4, commanded by Cpl R. T. Deering, a baker from Camberwell, lasted two hours longer than that.

Some of the tanks came in towing anti-tank guns and, as soon as they stopped, the guns were unhitched and manned either by personnel who had ridden in on the backs of the tanks, or who were brought out in armoured cars.

Like so many battles, it was a confusing picture for any commander wanting to follow the progress of the fighting. There were no communications and smoke from burning vehicles mingled with the dust and sand to send a huge brown cloud hundreds of metres into the air over the desert. It was almost impossible to pin down anyone in such conditions. Then, as soon as the full heat of the day clamped down, the mirages appeared, turning the landscape and anything that moved in it (when it could be seen through the dust), into a a shimmering, amorphous blur.

About 300 German infantry had followed the tanks across the perimeter, apart from those whose task appeared to be to lob grenades into the weapons pits from the backs of the AFVs. They were subjected to merciless fire from the artillery and a machine-gun detachment, and many scattered if they still could, trying to take cover in the nearly featureless country to the west of Bianca.

Some of these infantry advanced on R5 under cover of a small ditch and one of the defenders, Corporal L. H. Gazzard, a schoolteacher from the Victorian town of Bostock's Creek, stood up above his weapon pit to fire at them. Before he fired a single shot he was mown down possibly, as the official historian described him, 'a living symbol of utmost valour'; or more realistically, in a rather reckless move that weakened the strength of that little garrison at a time when it needed every man.

There was still no sign of the Italian infantry in spite of it being normal procedure for them to follow the tanks in. Spowers noticed this at once, but could find no explanation. It was only when Rommel's papers were found later that the explanation came to light. 'With the British artillery sweeping the whole area, the Italians crept under their vehicles and resisted all their officers' attempts to get them back.'

There were still pockets of resistance which achieved more than the rather dramatic and futile act of Cpl Gazzard. Cpl F. C. Aston, who was awarded the Military Medal for his bravery and example, was commanding a gun of the 24th Anti-Tank Company when he knocked out first a German Mk III and then two other tanks before being swamped by at least a dozen others which came to their rescue. Even when two of the gun crew were seriously wounded, he kept firing until the gun was smashed by a direct hit.

The weight of the attack fell next on the left flank, or the eastern side of Ras el Medauuar, where Rommel was pushing eastwards along the perimeter to open up the gap that he had already exposed. R5 was surrounded and its weapon pits blown in although it held out for several hours until 1 p.m. After leaving three tanks at R5, the head of the armoured column pushed on until it was in a position east of R7. There the tanks formed a semicircle facing east, while other tanks busied themselves by breaking down more of the wire. They cleared it like a grazier ridding himself of timber by linking a long chain between two of the tanks and then moving them forward together.

The defenders in R8, who were almost closer to the tanks than R7, opened fire on them with Boyes anti-tank rifles, light machine-guns and rifles, and the tanks withdrew at about noon. But it was only a short respite. An hour later they came back in even greater numbers and twenty-five of them formed a semi-circle around R8 and R9 and just sat there, very disconcertingly for the men inside the posts. They sat there for nearly four hours and then, without firing a shot, mysteriously withdrew under cover of their own artillery fire.

At about 11.30 the Allied tanks finally arrived to join battle. The spearhead of the German attack had come to a standstill, for the second time quite unprepared for the strength of the resistance. Now the enemy tanks found themselves being attacked by the Cruisers of the 1st Royal Tank Regiment, ten of them in all. They began firing at the enemy from a range of 700 m and were immediately rewarded when one medium and two light German tanks took a direct hit and started to burn.

The enemy put down smoke to cover their retreat and to rescue the crews from the three stricken tanks, and they fired back through the smoke in the direction of the British. As much by luck as skill, they scored a direct hit, in retaliation, on one of the

Squadron Commander's tanks which was destroyed within minutes after catching fire; and they hit two of the Cruisers as they turned right along a minefield to withdraw.

On Morshead's instructions the guns of the 1st and 107th Royal Horse Artillery then concentrated on the German armour until it was forced to withdraw behind Ras el Medauuar. It was the first sign that, against all odds, the defenders might yet still hold the upper hand.

▲ Brigadier R. W. Tovell, 26th Infantry Brigade. (20802)
◀ Brigadier A. H. L. Godfrey, 24th Infantry Brigade. (20726)

▲ An offensive patrol of Cruiser and light tanks leaves the fortress to take the battle far behind the enemy lines. (9952)
◀ Brigadier J. J. Murray, 20th Infantry Brigade. (20805)

▲ Elaborate dummy anti-aircraft posts confused enemy aircrews. (20798)
◄ German soldier captured inside the area of 2/32nd Battalion. (20744)
▼ Dummy planes made by Australian sappers. (20685)

▲ The utter desolation of the rugged east coast sector of the fortress, here guarded by men of the Australian Army Service Corps, fighting as infantrymen. (20693)

◄ Anti-aircraft gun position inside the fortress protected by Italian ammunition boxes filled with stones. They provided good protection against enemy splinter bombs. (7975)

▼ A 3.7-inch anti-aircraft gun in action at night. (20738)

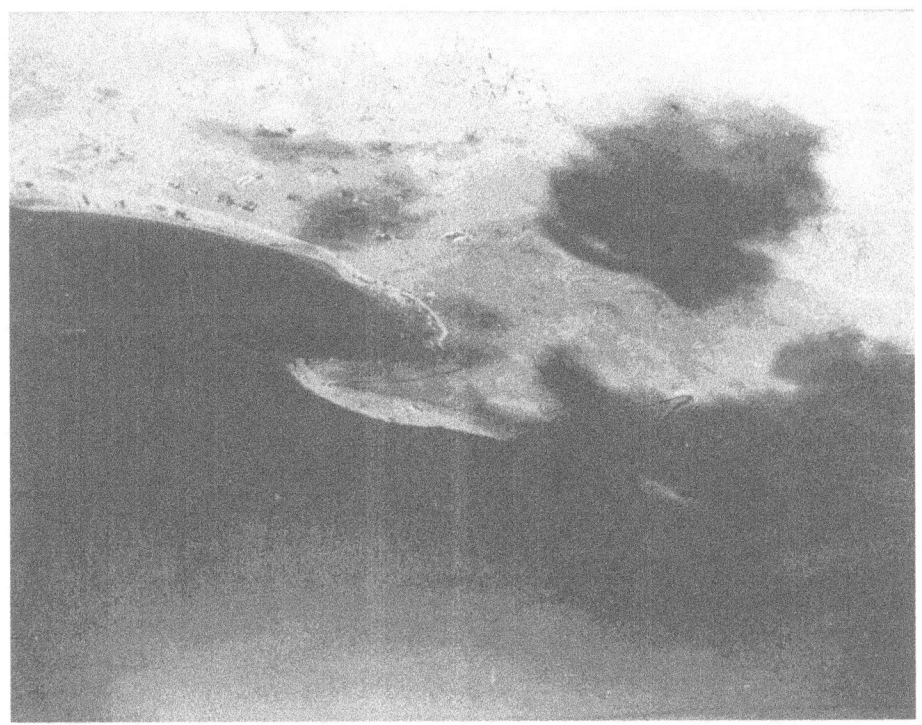

▲ The Port of Sollum and the vital pass (Hell-Fire Pass) carrying the road from the coastal plain to the top of the escarpment. (5872)

◀ A party of Australians wind their way up a typical zig-zag track leading out of a *wadi*. (20619)

▼ The armed merchant cruiser *Chakla* sunk within hours of arriving in Tobruk harbour. (127950)

▲ Post R25 with typical firing pits and interjoining trenches, here manned by 2/13th Battalion. (128991)
◀ Anti-tank ditch on the Tobruk perimeter. (134346)

▲ Detail of Post R39. Posts R33-R35 in the background were breached by the Germans during the Easter attack. (128988)

◀ Marshal Italo Gariboldi and General Erwin Rommel. (42386)

▼ Aerial view of Tobruk after the Italian surrender. The Italian cruiser *San Giorgio* burns in the background. (106640)

▲ Transport repair shop in need of its own repairs. (41847)
▼ The end of a German tank. (42011)

'Your Magnificent Defence...'

By the end of the morning, the Germans held the high ground around Ras el Medauuar and about 2000 m of the perimeter on either side of it — as far north as s9 and s8. Seven tanks had been positioned 600 m further north even than this, astride a track that led down over the edge of the escarpment to the Derna Road and the coast. From there they could fire on any patrols or reinforcements that came up the escarpment towards the salient, the inroad that the Germans and Italians had made into the fortress area.

Attempts to take s13 and s15 had been repulsed and Rommel made no further attempt at this time to extend his flank beyond s9, which managed to hold out.

Early in the afternoon, Morshead called Brigadier Tovell to Divisional Headquarters and ordered him to mount a counterattack, supported by tanks, with the aim of recapturing all the territory lost in the Medauuar sector. The attack was to be launched that same afternoon and it was to be carried out by Windeyer's 2/48th Battalion which was still in reserve since its relief by the 2/24th.

Windeyer was glad at last to have something concrete to do, but by 3.30 the counter-attack had been cancelled because the armour was urgently required to deal with German tanks that had been found forcing their way eastwards inside the perimeter.

Five Matildas, which were Infantry tanks, and three Cruisers advanced along the perimeter between the outer and inner posts. They made no attempt to conceal their presence, which would have been almost impossible anyway, and they drove straight for the enemy tanks, or where they had been told the enemy tanks would be.

They reached R11 and R12 by four o'clock and found that the Australians there had scarcely been troubled by the enemy; and then moved back towards R8 and R9 about 1000 m away where they believed the Germans were waiting for them. There were Australians in these posts, too, but here it was a very different story. They had been violently attacked and many of the men in the post had been wounded, some grievously. But the Germans had already gone, heading back, they were told, for the safety of Medauuar.

The tanks, apart from two of the Matildas which were left to protect R8, then moved still further to the west to R6, where again the Australians were found to be holding out. But now they had caught up with the German tanks, four of whose light tanks they could see near R5, while a medium tank was beside R4, both of which were already in the possession of the enemy.

They watched through binoculars as a staff car drove up to the four tanks. Four men, apparently the tank commanders, climbed on to their vehicles and disappeared from view. The British commander who was in one of the Cruisers, then ordered another Cruiser to attack the German medium tank at R4, but he had not looked over his shoulder. It had scarcely begun its approach when fourteen German medium tanks suddenly appeared from the rear and opened fire at 1000 m. Three of the Matildas hurriedly slipped round R6 and advanced to meet them, but at the same moment the commander's tank was hit and slewed to a standstill. The crew hastily abandoned it and rode to the safety of R8 on the back of the adjutant's tank.

Meanwhile the other two Matildas had been ordered to join in the hopeless attack on the fourteen medium tanks, an exercise that was a futile waste of human life and, almost more important at that critical time, of armoured fighting vehicles. By the time the short-lived and one-sided exchange was over, only one Cruiser and two Matildas were able to limp back to safety.

The German tanks, hardly inconvenienced by the skirmish, then turned away to other objectives and began shelling R6 and R7 into submission. R7 managed to hold out but R6, where all the automatic weapons had been destroyed by enemy fire and half the garrison of fourteen were casualties, surrendered at 7.30 p.m.

Post R7 was now completely isolated, cut off from food and water and surrounded on all sides by the enemy. Its situation was so desperate that, when no activity was spotted there for some hours, Windeyer assumed that it had been captured. But the Germans knew otherwise and at dusk they brought in a flame-throwing tank to crush the defenders inside the post once and for all.

The tank sat almost on top of the post and threw flame at it continuously, in a succession of bursts, for half an hour. The range was less than 10 m and the sheet of flame, scorching at the concrete, was 3 m high, but still the men inside defied the enemy. All night the tank remained there to prevent an escape, but fired no more flame or ammunition, and in the morning the corporal in charge of the post, Cpl K. S. Jones, a tough labourer before the war, made a hurried and hazardous reconnaissance of the situation by sticking his head out for about ten seconds. It was more than long enough, though, and realising the futility of trying to hold out longer, which could have had only one possible ending and no tactical advantage, he surrendered.

Rommel met them, too, as they marched off into captivity and after congratulating them in English, wished them luck until the war ended. As for many of the Allies, though, their imprisonment would be a hard ordeal, marked often by deprivation, overcrowding and brutality.

Sergeant Oakley in R9 had watched the four light German tanks form up and then attack R8, but for the moment at least, they left his own post alone. With no telephone or wireless he decided to send a runner across to R8 to assess the situation and see what state the garrison there was in.

It was a hazardous mission for there was a tank sitting almost on top of R8 and the runner was under fire almost the whole way across. By dodging and running in a zig-zag manner, however, he succeeded in reaching R8 unscathed. He found the commander there, Lt R. J. Gray, and a few others, uninjured but most of the men had been injured, some seriously. Gray told him that he would evacuate the post if he could get the injured out, but that there was little that R9 could do to help. The runner returned the same way he had come, taking advantage of an artillery barrage which had just started.

He was back in his own post by 6 p.m., just as the others were leaving to move to the relative safety of R11. They had no water and they were almost out of ammunition. As they made their escape, they looked across to R8 and could clearly see Gray getting into one of the British tanks. They assumed that he would be the last to leave and that the other members were either in the tank or had already been evacuated under cover of the same barrage.

Even as they watched, they saw three British 'I' tanks, the same Matildas that had futilely attempted to take on the German mediums, being repeatedly hit by enemy shells and immediately burst into flames. Helplessly they moved on. They had no time to lose if they were to reach safety themselves and there was nothing they could have done to help. They assumed that Gray must have perished in the tank. In that, at least, their fears were groundless for Gray escaped from the tank and survived the war.

After replenishing their water and ammunition at R11, they returned to R9, taking with them a unit from the 2/1st Pioneer Battalion which suddenly appeared as they were leaving. Once again the gods favoured them as they scurried back to their old positions and they made the hazardous 750 m dash without suffering casualties. They managed to hold out all through another night and they only surrendered the following afternoon after a bitter fight, in the course of which they destroyed a German flame-thrower that had been brought up behind a tank to flush them out.

They had noticed with satisfaction that there were many dead Germans on the ground outside R8 and they had caused many casualties themselves.

Towards the end of the afternoon, Morshead told Tovell that the counter-attack to recapture the lost perimeter, which he had cancelled earlier in the day, was on again and that the 2/48th was to prepare to move immediately. It would be replaced temporarily on the Blue Line by the 2/10th which would be brought back from its position at the junction of the Bardia and El Adem roads.

Tovell passed the message to Windeyer, in command of the 2/48th, who went immediately to see Spowers of the 2/24th, then requested that the assault be postponed until the following morning. It was impossible, Windeyer told his brigadier, to assemble his troops in time when they were spread over kilometres of the Blue Line. Many of them would not even have arrived at the start line by the time they had to leave.

Tovell said that he would refer it to Morshead and shortly afterwards Morshead himself came on the line and told Windeyer forcefully that it was essential that the assault take place that same evening. Again Windeyer repeated that, whether it was essential or not, it was physically impossible to bring all his battalion back when they were so scattered. But the GOC was not to be moved and, apart from promising transport to ferry the battalion back, he insisted that the plan go ahead that day as ordered. Windeyer promised that his men would do their best and asked for tank support.

Windeyer's orders were to recapture the perimeter between S7 and R5, an enormous task involving a distance of more than 4000 m that included twelve heavily fortified posts, all protected by barbed wire, landmines, booby traps and, most critically, German troops who would resist bitterly any attempt to remove them.

It would have been a difficult enough assignment for two battalions, reinforced by twenty or thirty tanks, and then only if the posts had been held by Italians. Windeyer was given one additional company from the 2/24th which meant that he had just four companies and one of these, on Morshead's instructions, had to be positioned on the Acroma Road facing south to deal with any enemy troops who slipped round from behind Carrier Hill.

Even with the transport that Morshead provided, there was barely time to get the whole battalion to the starting place on schedule. There had been no reconnaissance and no detailed planning. Simplicity was obviously going to be vital in the orders that Windeyer gave, for the opportunities for confusion and error were frightening. He therefore used the fact that they would be trying to recapture the same ground that they had been defending before they were relieved by the 2/24th. They would be going on to ground that they already knew and would recognise.

The first Company, led by Captain Woods, would advance along the right of the Acroma Road and seize S7 and S3. Captain Tucker's Company would follow 600 m behind Woods and its primary role would be to reinforce the final attack on Ras el Medauuar. Major Loughrey's Company would advance on the other side of the Acroma Road from Woods and would recapture all the posts between R2 on the left shoulder of Medauuar and R5 on the road running south-west out through the perimeter. The fourth company, on loan from the 2/24th, would occupy the battalion's old reserve position on Forbes' Mound and face south, to meet Morshead's special instruction.

The operation got off to a bad start even before they reached the pre-attack assembly area near Bianca. The transport to move them there never arrived and other trucks had to be hastily requisitioned. They were attacked by low-flying enemy aircraft all the way to the rendezvous, causing the trucks to scatter and one of them blew up, fortunately without loss of life. They finally arrived at Bianca more than half-an-hour late, in a choking duststorm, with no time for detailed briefing and had to move off into the glare of the sand-laden setting sun.

Nobody had told, or had been able to tell, the artillery of the delays in starting so that the guns began their bombardment at the pre-arranged time which was nearly half an hour too soon. The enemy, alerted by the bombardment that something was happening and with ample time to prepare for whatever it was, began shelling the leading companies almost as soon as they moved off.

Woods's plan was to attack S7 first and then mop up the other posts as he moved south towards the ultimate objective, Ras el Medauuar. But long before he reached S6, in the inner line of perimeter posts, he was pinned down by heavy machine-gun fire.

Woods had unintentionally been moving too far to the right in the valley that he was following, so that he was actually coming close to S8. Believing that S10 was still held by Australians, he sent out a platoon to come round on the flank and silence the machine-gun; but no sooner had it come within range of S10 than it found itself coming under vicious fire. In fact S10 *was* still held by the Australians, but it was completely surrounded by Italians, who were doing the firing. Unaware of this, the platoon commander, cursing Australians who fired on their own men, made a hurried change in direction.

A carrier patrol, which was supposed to be drawing the enemy machine-gun fire on itself so that its exact position could be pin-pointed, found instead that it was being attacked by anti-tank guns and tanks marooned in the minefield. It, too, after being severely ruffled was forced to make a hurried withdrawal.

Major Loughrey's Company, on the south side of the Acroma Road, quickly found themselves on the track that would bring them out near their allotted target on Ras el Medauuar. They heard tanks coming up behind them, not far away, but invisible in the sandstorm that was now raging. That, at least, was reassuring for they had worried that the promised tank support might never materialise.

The noise of the tanks grew louder, until they were no more than 30 m away and moving only a little faster than the men on foot. And then, in a sudden break in the dust, they did see them — flying the black swastika.

They did not even have time to react before the dust curtain closed again, shutting off that paralysing sight. But the tanks didn't seem to be reacting either. Perhaps the impossible had happened and the tank commander thought the men he must have glimpsed to his right were Italians, or even fellow-Germans. The tanks could be heard accelerating slightly as they pulled away. It must be all right. For once fortune was with them. And they were still reassuring themselves when the tanks suddenly wheeled in unison and came straight back towards them, firing into the dirt as they came.

They fell to the ground, vainly searching for some cover that would shelter them, but there was nothing. No cover, no shelter, no weapons that would halt the tanks and no protective tank within earshot. Loughrey didn't even have a wireless to call up help and he sent back a runner. In the meantime, he ordered a rapid withdrawal.

Over on the right, Woods had problems of his own, not least that he was still pinned to the ground by very accurate machine-gun fire that he had been unable to silence. He, too, sent a runner back to Windeyer, and the runner met Tucker, the commander of the company, following Woods 600 m behind, and gave him a hurried summary of what he knew. Eventually, the runner reported to Windeyer, Windeyer reported to Tovell and Tovell relayed his request to Morshead that the assault be postponed until the next day as they were most unlikely to make much more progress that night and still be back in cover by first light. But Morshead refused to consider it. The attack must go on.

Tucker, who was now catching up with Woods, advanced very close to the road so that he would not lose his direction. At the same time Woods was trying to encourage his platoons to move forward in short leaps and bounds, going ahead first on his own and then calling the platoons to follow him. It was a brave, if suicidal, gesture.

The first platoon ran straight into fire as it tried to execute its first bound. The platoon commander was wounded, two men were killed and so many of the others were injured that the platoon was to all intents finished as a fighting unit.

Undeterred, Woods called the second platoon to follow him and this time it was led by a sergeant, a former farmer, called Tonkin. He was shot dead almost before he could take a step; one of his sections was decimated with most of its men finished as fighting troops, and the platoon was left in total disarray.

By now Tucker had caught up and after a quick conference with Woods, they agreed to press on, although neither man had any idea what they were actually pressing on towards. The next two sections had more success and at least survived the great leap forward that Woods had devised for them. But immediately they came under machine-gun fire that seemed to be firing along fixed lines.

Woods, a printer by trade, was not lacking in guts, whatever other shortcomings he may have had as an officer. Taking his company sergeant-major and two runners with him, he crawled forward to fix the precise position of the machine-gun nest so that he could make a bayonet charge on it, ordering one of the surviving platoons to stay close behind. He could hear talking in the post, German not Italian, but he couldn't find it and he continued to crawl around with the other three men.

They must have been making a considerable amount of noise because a German called out loudly in English, inviting them to surrender. Immediately one of Wood's men hurled back some obscenity and they heard the Germans laugh before a vicious burst of machine-gun fire was loosed at them. It hit Woods and one of the runners, wounding them both severely, but when the sergeant-major came forward to help him, Woods sent him first to tell the platoon commanders to risk no more lives and to withdraw. Tucker agreed with alacrity and at 9.30 they began to work their way back.

All the time the Germans, not 100 m away, were taunting them and egging them on to surrender. The sergeant-major and one of the platoon commanders dragged Woods back, but he was beyond help and died early the next morning.

In the 2/48th's War Diary there is a note, 'This morning Captain

H. A. Woods died of wounds. Nothing more need be said than that we are all very sad and his men affected more deeply than words can tell. The soldiers thought him the finest of men.' The real tragedy was that his life and all the other lives that were taken and shattered in that futile exercise that evening were so needlessly wasted.

About the only success that was chalked up that night was won not by Windeyer's men, but by the 2/23rd Battalion further to the right. There, at least, a good number of Italians were killed or taken captive and anti-tank guns and small arms captured.

Windeyer reported his failure to Tovell who in turn relayed it to Morshead. In fact the information came as no surprise to Morshead who had been kept briefed by artillery observation officers at the front. It had been a foolhardy mission from the start, ill-prepared, ill-conceived and persevered with against the best advice of all his senior officers who were to be involved. The force he sent was woefully inadequate for the task they were set.

Morshead's immediate priority now was to prevent the enemy from sweeping forward from the positions that they were holding. There was little separating them from Fort Pilastrino, his own Headquarters, and the Derna Road which would take them into Tobruk town itself and the harbour.

With Tovell and Lt Colonel A. D. Verrier, who commanded the 2/10th Battalion which had taken over the defence of the Blue Line, he worked out a plan for forming a switch line to hold the now highly vulnerable gap between S8 and Bianca, behind which Windeyer had now moved his battalion with its very shattered morale. This switch line would link up with another switch line being prepared by Brigadier Murray who was commanding the 20th Brigade. Murray's switch closed the gap that had been opened up by the penetration on the eastern side of Ras el Medauuar. The switch lines were simply alternative defence lines which could be moved or switched to if a sudden change of tactics was required.

Verrier, who later in the war became Inspector of Military Prisons and Detention Barracks, came close to finding himself in precisely the same invidious position as Windeyer, of having to execute a complicated and important move without preparation or forethought.

As he left Morshead's headquarters early on 2 May, the wind was coming up and with it the dust. It was about two o'clock in the morning and pitch dark, and his vehicle went slower and slower until it could make no further headway in the deep sand. He decided to proceed on foot, for his battalion had to move at first light and he was carrying their orders with him.

He left the truck and set off into the darkness and the swirling dust that stung his eyes and whipped against his face and skin. By the time he arrived at his lines it was already four o'clock and the battalion was standing to arms. He had just two hours to issue his orders, explain to his officers the battalion's new role of linking S8 with Bianca and get the men moving.

There had been no reconnaissance and every move had to be by map and compass. The risks of another dangerous mistake through lack of planning were all too clear, but Verrier's luck held better than had Windeyer's and, by six o'clock all his companies were moving to their new positions. By half past, the move had been completed.

Casualties among the main body had been gratifyingly few and only in the outlying sections was serious resistance encountered. Close by a water tower near S6, Lieutenant Macfarlane and a party of men were attacked and pinned down and almost all of them were killed. Macfarlane himself survived and he made his way back, carrying a badly wounded lance-corporal.

They had reached Forbes' Mound and Macfarlane was staggering on under the weight of his load, when he suddenly realised that they were not alone. Standing across his path was a German soldier, astride a motor-bike and eyeing him quizzically. Had the German chosen to shoot, he would have been a defenceless target; had he been ordered to carry the wounded man into captivity, he doubted whether he could have managed another dozen steps.

Instead, the German did neither. He gave a quick nod of his head, a smile and then drove off, leaving Macfarlane and the soldier to finish their journey unharmed.

The positions which had been allotted on paper were not all as satisfactory on the ground, and there was a good deal of shuffling and reorganising by the commanders on the spot which Morshead was told about after the event. Some units found themselves on the wrong side of a mound, for example, while in other places the line was left entirely undefended. It was not Morshead's fault in his concept of the plan, so much as tired, confused individual commanders who shifted the positions allocated to them if they seemed to be weak, without thought for the overall result.

By morning the salient was ringed by the defending troops and if the barrier they put up against further advance by the enemy was not as strong as the original Red Line, it was at least certain that the enemy would have to fight for every inch of additional ground that they coveted.

The night had been unexpectedly quiet and the most serious incident had occurred near R10. There had been a heated discussion between the Commander of the 26th Anti-Tank Company and the senior officer of a company of Pioneers. The anti-tank man, an officer called Sheehan, was firmly of the belief that the line they had formed should be 1500 m further forward and a platoon of his company was sent forward to put its guns into the position.

Every move they made, however, had been carefully watched by the enemy and within an hour the gun positions had been overrun and the entire platoon except the Platoon Commander and seven men, who had been out on patrol, were captured.

The rest of that day, 2 May, was notable for how little fighting took place. The opposing artilleries duelled and forward observation officers in carriers constantly patrolled the battlefield looking for suitable 'opportunity' targets. Most of them had become so expert that they could bring their gunfire down on a small target with such precision that they often needed no ranging shots before they were hitting the target.

Once or twice there was evidence that the enemy were preparing to mount a limited attack, but each time they were quickly challenged and withdrew. Once a flame-thrower was brought up, protected by a carrier on each side of it, and was at once engaged by a Boyes rifle which set it on fire.

In an incident that nearly cost a sergeant his life, then ended with a display of heroism that won him the Distinguished Conduct Medal, a bren-gun carrier patrol had gone out to aid a unit of Pioneers who were in danger of being surrounded. Before the patrol could get close, however, it came under fierce small-arms fire which killed one man and wounded another.

They were on the point of withdrawing when one of the carriers broke down and was left stranded in open country with enemy fire pouring down on it. Sergeant J. W. Christsen deliberately reversed his own carrier up to it and with no thought for his own safety, leaped out and, momentarily protected by the two vehicles, attached a tow rope. Getting back into his own carrier was even more hazardous because now the enemy was waiting for him, but he succeeded and then dragged the broken vehicle and its crew back to safety.

Christsen, a builder's labourer from Queensland before he had an opportunity to show his talents as a leader, was promoted to Warrant Officer shortly afterwards only to be killed six months later.

The weather was insufferably hot and practically every day strong ground winds produced the blinding duststorms that brought all activity to a standstill. Men had to shout above the wind, visibility was almost nil, and life was just wretched. But all the time a watch still had to be kept in case the enemy might be tempted to launch an assault through the dirt.

Only the artillery was relatively unaffected by the duststorms because the shimmering mirages made ranging impossible when it wasn't dusty. On 2 May each gun of the 1st Royal Horse Artillery, for example, fired 900 rounds.

Morshead was determined to renew his attempts to recover the ground that had been lost and again the task would be given to the reserves who were held for precisely this purpose. He conferred with Brigadier Wootten who, apart from Chief of Staff Lloyd, was his most trusted adviser, and Wootten spent the day with the 20th Brigade (his own brigade was the 18th) bringing himself up-to-date with the relative positions of both sides.

He chose to launch his attack at night and Morshead gave details at a conference at his Headquarters on the morning of the 3rd. All three battalions of Wootten's 18th Brigade were to take part, the 2/9th, 2/10th and the 2/12th. The 2/9th, commanded by Lt Colonel J. E. G. Martin, would approach the salient along the perimeter fence from the left of Ras el Medauuar, stopping when it reached R1.

The 2/10th would approach from the right, also following the perimeter, and would mop up each post it passed until it, too, reached Medauuar. The battalion commander, Lt Colonel J. Field, a university lecturer in mechanical engineering, was probably a better administrative officer than he was in the field. The 2/10th, under Colonel Verrier, would push forward in the centre.

The artillery would support them and, to avoid shelling their own troops, would follow a very carefully worked-out programme. They would put down a barrage ahead of the advancing battalions and would keep just ahead of them, moving towards the first occupied position at a speed of 100 yards every three minutes. While the infantry disposed of that position, the artillery would turn its attention on the second post and would blast that for 90 minutes, and so on. Lesser targets could be pin-pointed and tackled as they were pointed out by the forward observation officers. It clearly called for very fine tuning.

Nineteen tanks would be available for the final kill or to come to the infantry's assistance, and the start time was fixed for 7.33 p.m. which Wootten later changed to 8.45 p.m. so that the enemy would not see the infantry moving into position. Unlike the two earlier unsuccessful exercises, this one at least was preceded by careful reconnaissance.

May 3 was a comparatively easy day for the infantry. The occasional attack by the enemy was tackled by the artillery or the machine-gunners and for much of the morning the most noisy fire was directed at Italians and Germans who were lifting mines from a minefield in front of Ras el Medauuar. An enemy machine-gun position near a white house between R7 and R8 was particularly troublesome and resisted every attempt to destroy it.

The assembly area selected by Wootten was in a *wadi* beside a track known as Fig Tree Road due east of and about 2000 m distant from S13. The slender moon, still in its first quarter, was very low in the sky and it was also slightly overcast so that the counter-attack began in pitch darkness.

There were a few casualties before they moved off, when artillery shelling, probably not specifically aimed at them, landed in the *wadi*. Most of the injuries were to members of the 2/12th because the 2/9th was half-an-hour late arriving.

First to move, on time, was the 2/12th. It passed through the lines of the 2/10th to get over to the right and immediately came under fire on both flanks from machine-guns in the salient and outside the perimeter. How the enemy knew exactly where they would be and when was never made clear, but their line of fire was perfect.

The Australians threw themselves to the ground, crawling and scuttering for whatever cover they could find. In the noise and the darkness, many of them became separated and their officers and NCOs tried in vain to collect them. Some found themselves right on the perimeter wire and crawled through it near S7, making for the cover of the anti-tank ditch, while others finished up near S6 by following a pipe-line ditch that they found themselves in. Many more got completely lost.

For four-and-a-half hours this chaotic situation continued while the withering fire from the machine-gun nests continued remorselessly. Half-an-hour after midnight one of Field's companies, which had remained fairly intact, was ready to storm S6 and S7 provided the artillery could neutralise the machine-gun fire for long enough to allow them to make their assault. But the artillery needed too long to make their calculations and Field didn't have that time to spare. Eventually it was agreed that, at 1.15 a.m., a general bombardment in the area of the machine-guns, rather than aiming specifically at the machine-gun nests, would begin and would last for fifteen minutes.

The company prepared to move and the bombardment started on time, but it made not the slightest impression on the machine-guns which continued with their deadly fire. By 1.30 Field was forced to report to Wootten that he had failed completely and that many of his men were still missing.

Over on the left, the 2/9th was trying to make up the half hour that it had lost by arriving late. The artillery programme had been amended, but in spite of that the guns were already firing when they started and the men moved out without even forming up properly.

Martin's orders required him to carry out his assault in two stages, the first to re-capture R8, R7, R6 and R5, in that order, as well as the white house near R8 from where the enemy was still directing machine-gun fire on the garrison; and the second to capture R4, R3, R2 and R1. Most of the infantry they would encounter would be Italians, it was believed.

They moved off to the same deadly greeting from enemy

machine-guns as the 2/12th had experienced, again from both flanks, and there was the same confusion. The enemy was also firing straight down the road on fixed lines. (When firing on fixed lines, the man handling the gun took no aim but simply fired it in a direction which had been fixed for him.) Fortunately the machine-gun was also firing tracer so its line of fire could be accurately picked out and avoided.

The company on the right of the 2/9th's advance was experiencing a problem that had not been anticipated. It found that the maps it was following to reach the posts bore no similarity to the ground itself. The road to R6, for example, as shown on the map, in fact headed off in a completely different direction.

The platoon going after R8 searched for it in vain and almost fell over a group of about eighty Italians who were sheltering behind a pile of stones. The platoon commander recovered first and ordered his men to charge with bayonets fixed after throwing in a few grenades. The result was gratifying with many of the Italians left dead or seriously injured and the rest put to flight.

Lt Noyes, who had led the bayonet charge on the Italians, took stock of his now depleted platoon but decided to press on in search of his real objective, R8. He had no sooner rallied his men together than he heard a rumbling along the track ahead of him and the next moment four light Italian tanks came trundling towards them. They jumped clear of the road and, as soon as the tanks were past, Noyes and his sergeant rushed out behind them, lifted the turret lids, pulled the pins from their grenades and dropped them in, slamming the lids behind them.

The effect was stunning and all four tanks burst into flames. It brought down a hail of fire, but Noyes and his little group had already moved on. Finally they reached what was clearly R8 and prepared for their assault — and then found themselves laughing aloud when they realised that it was quite empty and deserted.

The 2/10th in the centre was also faring quite well. It had the task of mopping up any enemy posts that were being by-passed by the other two battalions and they carried out a successful ambush that netted a German patrol of seven; and an assault with fixed bayonets, on a machine-gun nest which was captured without loss and with a great deal of screaming from the Italians inside when they found themselves facing the chilling steel of the bayonets.

This attack was led by a 23-year-old from South Australia, Lt F. W. Cook, who had been working as a laboratory assistant before he volunteered. He proved to be an absolutely fearless soldier and by the end of the war had risen to the rank of Lt Colonel and been decorated with both the DSO and the MC.

Cook's courage was infectious. A lance-corporal, sent out to try to find a missing patrol, came across a machine-gun post. Single-handed he charged into it, Tommy-gun blasting, and killed all six Germans in the gun crew. For this he was awarded the DCM.

There was no question that the assault was taking its toll and an Italian diary captured some time later spoke of the utter confusion that the Italians had been reduced to by the Australians. But at the end of the night, the overall position was little changed and the enemy had launched fierce counter-attacks and caused havoc of their own with their machine-gun fire.

The 18th Brigade reported ten dead, 121 wounded and twenty-four missing, a heavy toll when measured against the fact that the only post that the Australians now occupied which they hadn't controlled before the attack was R8, and the enemy had not even been in that when the assault began. The Germans and Italians together had lost thirty-six dead and 105 wounded. Another sixty-two were missing, mostly taken prisoner.

The one occupied post that came closest to being re-occupied was R7 where the Italians in possession of it were all killed or taken captive. But just before it fell, the enemy set fire to two blankets, hoping to deprive the Australians of the cover of darkness, and a tank and three German armoured cars hurried across to their assistance. They retaliated so fiercely that the Australians were forced to fall back and R7 reverted to the enemy.

For the third time in little more than twenty-four hours, an operation had failed in every important respect because it was ill-conceived and badly put together. Whatever the urgency for the occupied land to be taken back, at least as far as Morshead saw it, nothing altered the fact that he had given his battalions an impossible task. A task that, in spite of their best intentions and their unchallengable courage, had been attempted in a ham-handed and disorganised way that, at times, had proved as chaotic as anything the Italians put on.

To try to recapture, with just three infantry battalions and a handful of AFVs, eight fortified positions and innumerable secondary but deadly targets, over a distance of nearly 5000 m would have been a tall order at any time. To have to do it on a pitch-black night without a rehearsal and with almost no knowledge of where the enemy was or in what numbers, bordered on the foolhardy.

Churchill may have cabled the next day that 'the whole Empire is watching your steadfast and spirited defence of this important outpost of Egypt with gratitude and admiration', but for those first few days of May there were few gains from which Morshead could draw any satisfaction.

On the broader canvas, however, what was being achieved was that Rommel was learning very fast that this 'demoralised' force inside Tobruk Fortress, as he had rashly described it, was a very vicious enemy who, far from staying passively behind the barbed wire waiting to be overcome, was sallying forth with guns blazing and mounting an offensive on him! In this vital respect Wavell, in a signal to Morshead, was exactly right when he cabled, 'Your magnificent defence is upsetting the enemy's plans for the attack on Egypt and giving us time to build up a force for counter-offensive. ... Well done.'

It was a confusing time for the commanders on both sides of the perimeter. Each could reflect on splendid achievements and inexcusable failures but, on balance, as dawn broke on Friday 4 May (by which time Morshead had called back the 18th Brigade and cancelled the counter-attack) it was probably Morshead who had most reason to feel that the gods had chosen to favour him.

Stalemate

As May dragged on, the weather stayed hot and dirty and a thick film of dust covered everything that stayed motionless for more than a second. Swimming, and the chance to wash clothes in the warm Mediterranean, remained the greatest luxuries in an environment that was the ultimate antithesis of luxury in every other respect. The flies were a menace and hung over everything, from the latrines to the cook-house, like a black plague. About the only consolation for anyone inside the perimeter was that it was surely a hundred times worse for the Germans and Italians outside.

Any notion that Morshead entertained that he might be able to wrest the lost ground from the enemy was dispelled after the third counter-attack failed to achieve anything beyond reminding Rommel that he was fighting very tough soldiers with a formidably effective artillery to back them up.

The urgency now for the garrison was to strengthen the switch lines that had been hurriedly formed to keep the enemy inside the salient, and make them as strong, or hopefully even stronger, than the Red Line. To achieve this meant hard work by the engineers and a good deal of shuffling of manpower into new positions.

The 2/48th Battalion, still licking its wounds, took over the right of the new line; the 2/9th was moved to strengthen the centre and for the time being was transferred from the 18th Brigade's control to Murray's 20th. Each sector had previously been the responsibility of only two companies from other units.

There were some casualties in the course of the movements, most expensively from 2/9th Battalion which lost eleven dead, twenty-one wounded and two missing when Vernon occupied Bianca under deadly machine-gun and mortar fire. It was an important position to control, though, and it gave the Allies a valuable artillery observation post at what had been one of the weakest points on the line.

Rommel made one more effort to widen the breach in the perimeter, but after two hours of intense fire from artillery and machine-guns inside the wire, he withdrew. It was the last time he tried.

The days that followed were among the most strength-sapping and exhausting of the entire siege and as they turned into weeks, morale was weakened and sheer physical tiredness began to take its toll. Every spare moment of darkness was used to strengthen defences, but night patrolling had to go on as well in a constant endeavour to edge forward and re-take even a few metres of ground left carelessly unprotected by the enemy. At the same time, they had to fight off the enemy whenever he attempted to do the same thing. If rest had been possible when the night's exertion was over, it might have been bearable, but the day was too scorchingly hot to sleep and there was always, even on relatively quiet days, the unrelenting attention of the enemy artillery and dive-bombers.

The food they received was still drearily monotonous even if it was adequate to keep them working at the frenetic speed that Morshead demanded. In all the forward posts it had to be eaten hard, or uncooked, except for the one daily cooked meal which was brought forward after dark in hot boxes. The water was as disgusting to look at and taste as the German officer had described it in his diary when he wrote that it reminded him of sulphur-flavoured coffee.

Domination of no-man's land was still the cornerstone of Morshead's siege policy and it went on constantly, with no one excluded from involvement in some way. Whenever men came free from working on the extension of the new front, they were sent out on patrol, sometimes along the whole 34 km length of the outer perimeter, sometimes deep into the desert behind the enemy lines.

Inevitably there were times when the patrols came across the enemy unexpectedly or when they themselves were ambushed or followed. In one particularly savage attack, a platoon from the

2/23rd Battalion, led by former grocer's assistant Lt W. F. Brown, came across an Italian working party of more than eighty men. Most were unarmed, but the patrol gunned down fifty of them and returned with thirty-one prisoners. It was a brutal, if legitimate, act of war.

By mid-May the success of some of the small patrols had encouraged Morshead and his brigadiers to launch out on bigger and bolder assaults against the enemy, but it seemed once again that when anything too ambitious was attempted, it was doomed to fail.

Captain M. R. Jeanes of the 2/43rd Battalion was, beyond question, a very brave man. He finished the war with a DSO, an MC and an Efficiency Decoration to prove it. He also had the less enviable distinction of leading an attack on the enemy which failed in more respects than any other single operation of its size whose details are recorded.

His mission was simple enough. He was ordered to destroy some Italians who were dug in on the western side of the Belgassem *wadi* about 3 km outside the perimeter. Although they could be expected to put up much less resistance than if they were Germans, there were a great many of them close at hand, in fact three battalions between the head of the *wadi* and the Bardia Road.

The task was given to a company of the 2/43rd commanded by the 30-year-old Jeanes, a former health inspector. Supporting him were three troops of tanks, three armoured cars for communication between the infantry and the tanks; seven bren-gun carriers and an assortment of machine-guns, mortars and artillery. It was a good supporting cast.

Jeanes attempted to get the whole show under way on 13 May. In fact, it was a shambles. There was no coordination between any of the units and they all set off in different directions at various times. A carrier was sent to guide the tanks towards the *wadi*, but the driver got lost and went so far off course that he almost ran over his own infantry who were waiting to advance.

The tanks thought the infantry's arrival was the cue to start firing and they blazed away in half-a-dozen directions at once; the Italians, who until then had been dozing fitfully, thought the world had come to an end and also began shooting in all directions, pinning down the Australian infantry so effectively that they couldn't move; and Jeanes rushed around trying to restore some kind of order.

He eventually collected the carriers and told them to attack if necessary without his orders, a rash move indeed. At that moment someone in the enemy lines fired a Very light signal which, by ill coincidence, happened to be also Jeanes's signal for a general withdrawal. All his vehicles and those infantry who could move promptly started to head back for base. He was able to stop most of the carriers but the infantry had gone.

The tanks had, by this time, realised where they ought to be facing and the three infantry tanks, throwing caution to the wind, headed straight towards the Italians, spurning all cover, fearless of the wall of fire that was being directed at them. It would have served them better if they had shown a little fear, for two of them drove straight into the line of fire of anti-tank guns and were stopped in their tracks; the third, after running over two anti-tank guns rather than knocking them out, kept heading north until it was far beyond the Italians. The Cruiser tanks were withdrawn and taken out of range as soon as their commander realised that to proceed would achieve nothing but lose Morshead the services of six invaluable tanks.

Jeanes, who by now had about as much control over his men as he did over Rommel's Panzer division, tried to mount some kind of attack with his carriers and the handful of infantry who had not long since left the battlefield. Lt L. J. Pratt of the 2/43rd led the three carriers against the stronghold, but two were crippled within moments of appearing before the Italians and Pratt himself was killed. The infantry were once again so effectively pinned down that they couldn't move in any direction so Jeanes ordered them to withdraw.

Other carriers belonging to the Service Corps saw their predicament and raced across with the armoured cars to help and they, at least, met with some success. Under cover of smoke, which they laid down very fast, the infantry were able to withdraw and the surviving crews of the three infantry carriers were rescued.

For a short time, it seemed as though something of the assault might be salvaged, for the Cruiser tanks moved forwards to engage the enemy. But the anti-tank fire was still so deadly that they were forced to withdraw without causing any damage.

The whole farcical exercise was a textbook lesson in how not to wage war. As happened so often in the desert, it was shown that courage and enthusiasm were seldom sufficient to compensate for incomplete planning, inexperienced officers and a determined and heavily armed enemy.

Lessons in disarming and crippling tanks and other armoured vehicles were high on the priority list for newcomers to the desert. Accepting that a small .303 round of ammunition could stop a tank took time, but there were many instances in the desert when a rifleman or a bren-gunner found the Achilles heel and literally stopped a tank in its tracks.

The secret was in knowing where to find these vulnerable places. The big German 'I' or Infantry tanks, for example, had very thick turrets and even a 25-pounder shell could bounce right off them, and there were cases where the turret was undamaged — but blown clean off the hull. Their tracks, on the other hand, were a very weak spot.

The hull was also vulnerable and, on the Panzer II, the hull that was visible between the tracks as it approached was only 12 mm thick as opposed to 15-21 mm almost everywhere else. Men were taught, too, that the driver sat on the front left-hand side with the tank's massive gear-box on his right, so that only the left was very vulnerable, even to armour-piercing shells.

It was found by trial and error that six-wheeled armoured cars should be tackled by firing at the radiator, while eight-wheelers were weakest at the engine in the rear of the car. The driver's visor was always a weak spot. As the crew of the Italian tanks that were disabled during the counter-attack found out, it paid to keep the lid securely fastened from the inside.

Similar rather wishful orders were given to the troops for shooting down passing aircraft. The Junkers 87, for instance, was said to be ideally positioned for shooting down when it was diving straight at you or just pulling out. In these positions, the pilot was not protected by armour and there was no need to aim off to allow for the plane's speed.

The Messerschmitt ME110 which often escorted the Junkers became something of a jinx aircraft from the Allies' point of view. Rumours quickly spread that it was not only very fast, but had such an armoured cockpit that it was invulnerable. Only when a rifleman from a Pioneer unit unmistakeably shot down an ME110 did this complacency change, and inevitably, after that, others were destroyed in the same way.

Twice the Germans had deliberately attacked hospital ships flying Red Cross markings and during this period a third hospital ship, the *Karapara*, which had Red Cross markings everywhere and an enormous Red Cross flag at the forepeak, was attacked by twelve bombers which attacked her in waves of three.

There was no possibility of them having made a mistake because a reconnaissance plane had circled her closely and then flown off about half-an-hour before the attack. The *Karapara* did not sink, although there were a number of casualties, and the only explanation for what was not characteristic behaviour by the enemy in the Mediterranean, was that they feared that the Allies would use the protection afforded by hospital ships to get their troops out of the besieged fortress.

Other legitimate naval targets also joined the scrap heap of ships that now littered Tobruk harbour or went to the bottom on their way there. A minesweeper, the *Stoke*, was sunk by bombers who scored three direct hits; and the *Ladybird*, which had been living dangerously in the harbour as a floating gun battery for the army, was sunk six days later and went down with guns firing.

In spite of the abortive efforts to extend the ground that he held and recapture the perimeter posts now occupied by the Germans and Italians, Morshead insisted that this aggressive policy should continue. The opportunity for embarking on a new phase of his campaign arose when the jaded 26th Brigade was relieved on the edge of the salient by Wootten's 18th Brigade.

Wootten was a man after Morshead's own heart and the general knew that he would not spare his fresh troops in an effort to secure his objective. Unhappily, he seemed to have learned few lessons from the earlier debacles.

'Put in hand *at once*,' he underlined in his written orders to Wootten, 'a policy of aggression against the enemy; exert and maintain a superiority of morale over him; systematically wipe out his forward posts and occupy the same ground, and thus incessantly exert pressure against the enemy and relentlessly drive him back, bit by bit . . . It must be made perfectly clear to all ranks that we are not simply here to hold a line; but that we are here definitely for the purpose and intention of regaining ground previously lost and of inflicting loss on the enemy by every means in our power.' They were stirring words but they had little chance on past performance of ever becoming reality.

In the first week of May, a decision had been taken over the head of Morshead which made this task incomparably more difficult and hazardous. When he had been made to hand over all but a handful of the RAF aircraft based at Tobruk, because of fears that they would be quickly shot down by the enemy without making any significant contribution, he had been left relying on an army-cooperation squadron. This squadron flew the small tactical reconnaissance planes and also acted as invaluable airborne artillery observation posts. Now Morshead was told that he was to send this back to Egypt as well.

Morshead protested vigorously to Beresford-Pierse, the Western Desert Force Commander, but it made no more impression than had his earlier objections to losing the RAF. He had even been asking in vain for two months for air photographs of the desert around Tobruk so that he could know the dispositions of the enemy before launching an attack on them, but in all that time he had not received one.

Wootten's new responsibility for the western sector saw the start of a counter-offensive by the Allies that went on through the summer months and into August. At the cost of many lives, much suffering and questioning of objectives, some of the ground that had been lost to the enemy was gradually re-taken. Indeed some of it was re-taken, lost again and then captured for the third time.

As these spartan fortified posts, scratched-out holes in the dirt and patches of sand without any intrinsic value in themselves, were fought over and died for, there were some in the garrison — 'fifth columnists', Morshead called them — who wondered aloud what on earth they were doing it all for. And it was a reasonable question, for in spite of the supremacy that Rommel clearly had in some departments — most visibly in his tanks although, after his May defeat, he made much less use of tanks around Tobruk — there was a remarkable balance of power between the two sides.

The combination of Allied bravery, possession of the fortress, and the good line of supply that they enjoyed, nicely balanced the more powerful army that the enemy could field plus Rommel's brilliance. And the truth was that Rommel was not a brilliant commander when he was fighting positional battles, where his troops got down in one position and fought from there. It was in mobile warfare that his tactics were superb and he himself conceded willingly that he was never happy in the role of a foot soldier, slogging it out man against man.

So, hypothetically, if both sides had been content to bombard each other with their artillery and sit on either side of the wire waiting for the other to make a mistake, the results of the siege would probably have been much the same as they eventually turned out to be. What prompted the questioning was the constant suspicion that these bloody little skirmishes that took place all the time, yet seldom ended with any change in either side's relative position, took a terrible toll of life and achieved nothing.

The belief that Morshead wanted to foster was that the endless fighting and the appalling casualties were both necessary factors in making the enemy keep as large a force as possible at the perimeter.

One of the earliest tasks given to Wootten was to create a major diversion that would tie up Rommel's troops around the fortress while an assault was being carried out in the Salum area on the Egyptian border.

Churchill saw this operation, codenamed (appropriately, as it turned out) BREVITY, in characteristically melodramatic terms. It was designed, he wrote, 'to claw down Rommel before the dreaded 15th Panzer Division arrived in full strength from Tripoli.' In fact, as Wavell saw it, it was nothing of the sort.

It was primarily an exercise with the limited but vital objective of regaining the area around the frontier and particularly the Halfaya Pass. Morshead was encouraged to act quickly when he saw that Rommel's forces, away from Tobruk, were spread very thinly on the ground. If the Germans crumbled, he might be able to press on and mount a combined assault with the garrison that would drive the enemy out of that part of the desert to a safe distance west of Tobruk. But it was a pipe-dream. The Germans wouldn't crumble quickly, but would fight fiercely and, like his own troops in Tobruk, had the advantage of already being in possession.

What he wanted of the garrison in Tobruk, therefore, was a very fierce and noisy distraction that would keep Rommel's troops safely in position around the perimeter, while the attacking force slipped into Libya from Egypt.

Wavell briefed Beresford-Pierse along these lines and he, in turn, issued his instructions to Morshead on 8 May. Unfortunately, he posted them and the letter took five days to arrive in Tobruk. It was not the least of the factors that prompted Wavell, a little later, to make Morshead directly answerable to him instead of through Beresford-Pierse's Western Desert Force.

The letter arrived at the worst moment, just as Wootten was relieving the 20th Brigade at the salient. Morshead did the best that he could, however, and arranged a series of forays and operations all of which had a genuine purpose, however limited. At the same time, he would make a lot of noise and dust and give the impression that a full-scale attack had been mounted.

When the time came, he achieved this by moving convoys of trucks and tanks backwards and forwards inside the perimeter, kicking up clouds of dust. False radio and telephone messages were put out, Very signals were fired around the perimeter and the artillery stepped up the intensity of its bombardment.

Some of the assaults that were mounted were surprisingly successful, often because they yielded a horde of Italian prisoners instead of the handful which were expected. The Australians successfully attacked an enemy machine-gun nest on the escarpment near the Derna Road, killing two of the crew and wounding another two. They were content with that but suddenly, like wasps whose nest has just been broken, a whole crowd of other Italians appeared in nearby positions and began to throw off their coats and jackets. Then, unimpeded, they set off in a north-westerly direction, running as fast as they could.

That would have been pleasing enough for the Australians, who revelled in Italian cowardice, but they had not gone 300 m when another 150 Italians, startled by the sudden activity, jumped out of their trenches and stood up against the horizon to see what was happening. The Australians fired wishfully after them, but the 150 had already joined the flight. There were far too many to attempt to take prisoner so the patrol returned, for the cost of one man slightly wounded.

Morshead could not abide the idea that any of his positions might be given up without a fight and he was easily goaded. When a German prisoner lied under interrogation and said that his unit had captured S10 from the Australians without encountering any resistance and with none of the Australians being injured, he was furious. In a personal memorandum to his brigade commanders, which was intended equally for the battalion commanders, he complained that the number of casualties at S10 was too small. 'Rather a new experience for the AIF,' he said caustically of the fact that S10 and other posts had just been mopped up.

He coupled it with an order to improve the posts and make them more effective for their defensive role. Until that happened, 'they are just sleeping or funk holes and we shall lose more prisoners.'

Morshead had made no attempt to check out the prisoner's story and by the time the truth was relayed to him, the letters had gone out and the totally unfounded insult spread around the garrison that the unit which had been defending S10 was cowardly.

What actually happened was that the garrison in the post had put up bitter resistance against the Germans. Several of them had died during the fight and others were severely injured; the post was finally only overrun because they were unable to counter the fixed-line machine-gun fire that poured down into the weapon pits from higher ground.

Later S10 would be re-taken by the Australians when a strong fighting patrol raced across fire-swept ground to assault it. The patrol captured a German officer and twenty-six men, together with all their weapons. They freed two wounded Australians who had been held captive there. They had been well cared for by the Germans.

BREVITY, by common consent, was an almost total failure. The attacking force came nowhere near Tobruk and its sole achievement was that it left the Halfaya Pass in the hands of the Allies. But the towns of Salum and Capuzzo, which were briefly occupied, were recaptured by the Germans; and with Salum went the Salum Pass which was as tactically important as Halfaya.

There were plenty of Italian prisoners taken, but capturing them was no harder than swatting flies and they had become more of a nuisance than a bonus. They cluttered up Tobruk and they had to be fed. The Germans also lost three tanks, but the Allies lost five.

Among the other objectives selected during BREVITY was the recapture of S8 and S9, but this was abandoned when it was discovered that they were already occupied by Australians. With an alarmingly short time to go, the artillery bombardment which had been ordered to soften up both posts, was cancelled.

Lt Colonel Bernard Evans, commanding officer of the 2/33rd

Battalion and one of the most forceful battalion commanders in the desert, had been given the task of dealing with s8 and s9. Instead, he asked permission to be allowed to take s4, s5, s6 and s7 and quite regardless of the fact that it was an impossible task to set a single battalion, Morshead agreed.

As the 2/23rd set out, they were greeted by a very heavy artillery bombardment to which the British artillery responded in kind. They were being supported by tanks, but shortly after they crossed the startline, thick smoke was put down across Ras el Medauuar. The smoke combined with the dust and sand that were already being blown up, and visibility came quickly down to 50 m and then 25 m.

The tanks could not see where they were going, but still pressed on and then suddenly turned towards s9, mistaking it for s6, their objective. Fortunately for the Australians inside s9 the tanks did not open fire but just sat there waiting for further orders.

A platoon of infantry coming up behind realised what had happened and tried to attract the attention of the tank crews who had closed up their tanks. They beat on them with rocks and rifle butts but to no avail and nobody had told them that at the back of all the tanks was a button which rang a bell inside the tank to attract the attention of the commander. The infantry moved on to the correct post without them and eventually, the tanks took it on themselves to go back to the assembly area when it looked as though nothing was going to happen at s9.

Let down by the tanks, which should have been beside them, and suffering heavy casualties from 88-mm shells that burst frighteningly in the air 15 m above their heads, the infantry plodded on towards the first of their objectives. Many were killed on the way there, many more died and were injured during the assault.

Some of the bitterest fighting of the whole siege occurred during the confused day that followed. Evans's battalion had 163 casualties, yet when the dust had settled, they had achieved nothing. He was extremely fortunate that his whole battalion was not wiped out as it came perilously close to being. As usual, communication between infantry and armour was all but non-existent, with the tanks giving the impression that they were there on a private war which was no concern of the infantry. To set as objectives the capture of S4, 5, 6 and 7 when one of them alone would have taxed them to the full, had been a bad decision, but Morshead made many such bad decisions when his obsession with offensive tactics overrode his common sense.

The belief that either BREVITY, or some other operation in the near future, would result in the relief of Tobruk, seems to have prompted some Quartermaster far from the battle scene to decide that rations and supplies could be substantially pruned. As a result, the men in the fortress had no fresh meat for nearly three months and no fresh fruit at all until a memorable day in June when each man was issued with one orange.

Compared with many of the other great sieges in history, lack of supplies was not one of Morshead's biggest worries. The Navy and a flotilla of little boats kept the garrison provisioned and supplied with ammunition and fuel with a bravery and devotion that equalled that shown at Dunkirk.

Everything came from Egypt, some in the fastest ships the Royal Navy could provide, some under sail. They were in constant danger of attack from the air, from patrolling enemy warships and from submarines. Captain Albert Poland — later, to the delight of more people than he could imagine had heard of him, Vice-Admiral Sir Albert Poland — was the commander of this motley collection of vessels that called itself the Inshore Squadron.

They lost many ships — a whaler, two minesweepers, a gunboat, a sloop, two armed boarding vessels and an anti-submarine trawler in the six weeks before 1 June alone; and four more were damaged in the same period.

They were crewed by men of all nationalities, Greeks and Levantines, British and Australians (a lieutenant in the Royal Naval Reserve, Australian A. B. Palmer skippered the schooner HMS *Maria Giovanni*), Poles and Slavs. Australian destroyers made regular runs into Tobruk and the sloop HMAS *Parramatta* was sunk by torpedoes off Tobruk.

Shortage of ammunition had therefore never been a serious problem and the assortment of guns in the Bush Artillery, those weapons of all shapes and sizes which had been seized from the Italians, had enough ammunition captured at the same time to last a dozen sieges.

But the decision to reduce the supplies being sent to the garrison included ammunition and suddenly, from their normal usage of about forty tons a day (much of it 25-pounder shells), they were having to economise down to a little more than five tons. It took very little time for the enemy to realise what was happening, when the 25-pounder crews were ordered not to fire more than ten rounds each per day, instead of up to 100 as before.

They stepped up their own bombardment and, guessing correctly that anti-aircraft ammunition would also be in short supply, increased their attacks with dive-bombers.

The logic of not bringing in too much ammunition was valid enough — if there was too much it could not be easily taken away, and if the fortress was overrun there was no point leaving it for the enemy — but the basic premise was wrong, that the garrison was going to be relieved in the first place.

As May moved into June, there had been another crisis, this time with fuel, although it was largely brought on by the garrison's own short-sightedness. Petrol was used for the first six weeks of the siege as though there was a bottomless refinery in the middle of the perimeter and daily consumption was about forty-six tons, well over 400,000 l a day. What Morshead did not know was that this was only being achieved by drawing heavily on reserves and not from regular deliveries.

The garrison would have run itself into serious trouble in any case, but the crisis came even earlier when a petrol dump was bombed and burned out, which in turn set alight a diesel oil dump which was close by. A fairly half-hearted attempt was then made to reduce the daily usage, but still there was no note of real alarm. Out of the blue on 2 June, Morshead was told that by the end of that day the garrison would have between it just 130 tons of petrol. That represented three days' usage on past performance, after which every petrol-driven vehicle, including many of the tanks, trucks and other AFVs, as well as pumps and generators, would come to a standstill.

Morshead was incensed that he had not been warned before and by the excuse that the situation had only occurred because of the bomb attack on the dumps and the sinking of two fuel-carrying ships bringing in 1100 tons.

He ordered drastic reductions to be made. No transport was to be used unless there was no other way of doing a job and, disastrously for morale, no more transport was to be used for taking the troops the 4 km to the beach. His target was to reduce consumption overnight to less than twenty tons a day.

There was hope of early relief when it was reported that a lighter, loaded with petrol and escorted by a minesweeper, was leaving Mersa Matruh for Tobruk, but the minesweeper was sunk and the lighter was too vulnerable to go on without escort. In the end salvation came with an old boat, the *Pass of Balmah*, which chugged its way down the coast at a top speed of six knots, surviving two attacks on the way, and finally made Tobruk safely. Heavily camouflaged in the harbour, she discharged 760 tons of bulk petrol.

This remarkable little vessel then turned straight round and went back to Alexandria, knowing that the fortress now had forty days' supply of petrol. Before the month was out she returned with a second delivery of another 700 tons.

Wavell was being constantly goaded by Churchill into attacking, no matter whether Wavell believed it imprudent or not, and the Prime Minister found him increasingly unsatisfactory as a commander. 'I am deeply disturbed at General Wavell's attitude,' he said in a minute to his Chiefs of Staff. 'He gives me the impression of being tired out.'

Churchill wanted one of his own generals to replace him and specifically he wanted Sir Claude Auchinleck, the Commander-in-Chief, India. But he seemed ambivalent about actually sacking him. 'Back him or sack him!' his CIGS, Sir John Dill, insisted, but Churchill could not see it in such black and white terms.

On 27 May, Churchill had issued to his Chiefs of Staff one of his minutes which many found inspiring and Wavell found irritating. 'In the Western Desert alone, the opportunity for a decisive military success presents itself,' he told them. (Alone, because the Allies had suffered a string of disastrous reverses, including the sinking of HMS *Hood*, many naval losses in the Mediterranean, and the failures in Greece and Crete.) 'Here the object must not be the pushing back of the enemy to any particular line or region, but the destruction of his armed force in a decisive battle fought with our whole strength. It should be possible in the next fortnight to inflict a crushing defeat upon the Germans in Cyrenaica.'

Wavell's answer to this demand for an instant battle was an operation which he code-named BATTLEAXE and which would have three principal objectives. It would defeat the enemy on the Egyptian frontier where Operation BREVITY had failed to shift them; it would defeat the enemy at Tobruk; and it would drive them far to the west until they were at Derna and Mechili, the scene of one of Rommel's most humiliating defeats early in the campaign.

Wavell warned immediately, to Churchill's disgust, that it was very doubtful whether BATTLEAXE would succeed. But in this he was wholly supported by the other two Commanders-in-Chief, Tedder of the Air Force and Cunningham of the Navy. Tedder said that little fighter support would be forthcoming; Cunningham that it was becomingly increasingly difficult to keep the fortress supplied, let alone an additional major operation that could last for many weeks; and Wavell himself believed that the Germans were likely to launch an overwhelming assault with their full Panzer strength at any moment.

There was no question, though, that BATTLEAXE would proceed, and all worked to that end. Unlike BREVITY, where the opening up of a corridor to Tobruk had never been a likely possibility, except possibly in Churchill's imagination (certainly not one that Wavell had seriously contemplated), BATTLEAXE relied heavily on the siege being broken for long enough to allow a force to get out and take its part in the defeat of the enemy.

As Rommel was now firmly entrenched in strong defensive positions all round the perimeter, any break-out would involve heavy casualties and considerable losses to the tanks and other AFVs. Timing was crucial, for if the garrison broke out too early and found that the main attacking force coming towards them from Egypt had been stopped by the enemy, the future defence of the fortress would be seriously compromised. It would be left undefended with the garrison on the wrong side of the gate. A reasonable extension of that scenario was that Tobruk would fall and Rommel would be excellently placed to begin his invasion of Egypt at his leisure. Patience was going to be Morshead's strongest card.

Operation Battleaxe

Tiger had delivered its long-awaited load of armour and BATTLEAXE was scheduled to begin on 15 June 1941. That allowed only a few days to prepare for it, an absurdly short time for the new tanks and their crews to become integrated and to prepare for a battle whose result, one way or the other, would have such important consequences.

Wavell would have chosen to wait, in spite of the impatience of Churchill. A far greater concern was that, with the defeat of the Allies in Crete, the Germans would have an air base with which they could threaten any shipping in the Mediterranean and protect their own convoys reinforcing the Africa Corps. Wavell could choose to delay and bring his troops up to a proper state of readiness, only to find himself facing an even more formidable German army. He opted to strike at the earliest opportunity.

Morshead's role was to keep the besieging army so occupied when the attack was launched over the Egyptian frontier, that it would be tied down at Tobruk, and unable to go to the assistance of the other Axis forces further east. He was not to burst out of the perimeter until the main force was certain of making contact with him and it was agreed that this situation would have been reached when it arrived at Ed Duda, a prominent hill 13 km southeast of the perimeter.

Rumour quickly spread through the garrison that a strong relieving force, with a lot of armour, was being formed to come to their rescue. It created a buzz of excitement and, in spite of all the secrecy that surrounded BATTLEAXE, it became the most talked about topic in the fortress.

The plan for the garrison was quite simple as Morshead outlined it. There would be a number of diversionary attacks at various points of the perimeter, including a landing by British commandos 10 km east of the Zeitun *wadi*, on the Egyptian side of the fortress. The commando company (which included Winston Churchill's son, Randolph) would come ashore behind the enemy lines and cause as much pandemonium as possible, and this would be reinforced by both the 24th and 20th Brigades opening fire from inside the perimeter.

As soon as the main force came within 33 km of Tobruk, it would send a coded message to GHQ which would be the signal for Wootten to lead his battalions out through the wire. There would be a fierce, but hopefully brief skirmish as they fought their way through the enemy positions outside the perimeter; and then the 2/9th and 2/12th Battalions would form a corridor, with the 2/9th at Bir Ghersa on the right and the 2/12th on the left.

Inside this zone, the supporting artillery would site its guns, and the third battalion, the 2/10th, would forge ahead and seize Ed Duda. It was to hold the hill until the arrival of the main force. The 2/10th was now a very mobile force, equipped with vehicles taken largely from the 18th Indian Cavalry Regiment.

Rommel's intelligence had been good and all pointed to the likelihood that Wavell was planning to seize the frontier and then drive west along the coast road, or across the desert, to relieve Tobruk. The Germans anticipated this brilliantly by staging a succession of ambushes and assaults, using machine-gun nests, artillery bombardments and, always, the Panzer. His 15th Armoured Division was now commanded by General Walther Neumann-Silkow, who was one of the outstanding armour commanders of the war.

At every stage of the battle, Rommel seemed to be uncannily aware of Wavell's next move. The Allies would arrive at a specific point and find the Germans or the Italians waiting for them; or they would site their artillery in a pre-arranged place and discover half a dozen machine-gun posts firing at them along fixed lines. This meant that they had been set up in the correct place even before the British got there. Rommel actually sent a detachment to Ed Duda, when it was still unoccupied and before any logical appreciation of the battle could have suggested that it had special significance over any other feature in the desert. It was as though the Germans had been given the Allied battle-plan.

After three days of often bitter fighting by both infantry and armour, BATTLEAXE had achieved almost none of its objectives and it had lost sixty-four of its 100 Infantry tanks and twenty-three of its ninety Cruisers. The operation was called off and the Allies limped back disconsolately to their original positions. The disappointment when news of the failure leaked back to the fortress was intense, but at least Tobruk was still secure. Churchill, who viewed the failure of BATTLEAXE as the last straw, at last got rid of Wavell and replaced him with Auchinleck.

Churchill wrote later that the operation had been 'ill-concerted', as he put it, 'especially from the failure to make a sortie from the Tobruk sally-port as an indispensable preliminary and concomitant.' Had Wavell done so, however, Tobruk would certainly have been lost and all that the garrison had achieved at such cost in life and stress would have been wasted. The Germans and Italians were hovering for the kill right round the perimeter and, if nowhere else, the place in the wire where Wootten's Brigade was going to force its way through, on the way to Ed Duda, would have been turned into an enemy bridgehead through which their armour and infantry could have poured unchecked.

Morshead was determined that the failure of the relieving force to get through was not going to undermine morale, which was already stretched to the limit. He was fast becoming a commander who was brave and resourceful — but never won battles. Except for small assaults and some successful long-range patrols, it often seemed as though nothing would ever budge the Germans. As one monotonous, dangerous day of stress, discomfort and frustration dragged into another it was easily forgotten that one of the most important tasks the defenders could perform, was being carried out to perfection. Tobruk continued to be denied to the enemy, in spite of all that Rommel could throw at it, and in that single fact, the Western Desert, the Middle East, indeed the whole of Europe, were that much safer.

It was a vital theatre of war, far more important than was suggested by a bombed-out Italian colonial town surrounded by miles of barbed wire on the edge of the most desolate desert in the world. But it was hard to convince men of that when they felt as though they were in a huge cage, being fired at, bombarded, bayoneted, mortared, attacked with hideous flame-throwers and cascaded with bombs filled with splinters that exploded 15 m above their heads. And when no relief was in sight.

Morshead countered this sort of defeatism by putting men to work and to fight, morning, noon and night, until they were too tired to think of anything else.

The enemy lost ground in the salient at the end of June when the 2/13th Battalion undertook the hazardous task of constructing new positions between Bianca and Ras el Medauuar in ground that was alive with booby traps and mines.

Work began on the night of 22 June and even before the evening meal had arrived three men had been blown up and wounded by a mine. At 1 a.m. three more men walked on a booby trap which killed two of them and seriously wounded the third. The explosion brought an immediate response from enemy machine-guns which fired down fixed lines on the 2/13th.

Before the night was out, ten more men were wounded and one killed in separate incidents. The following night, the work had still not been completed, and other units of the 2/13th went out into the minefield, moving very cautiously. They attempted to stay spread out, not bunched together, but two parties of Intelligence men and engineers, working towards each other from the flanks, came together in the centre. They were standing talking in a group when a booby trap went off under their feet. Four more men died and six were injured. An enemy mortar immediately opened up killing yet three more and injuring another six.

The lessons to be learned from these tragedies were quickly memorised and, although there were other victims of the booby traps and mines, there was never again the carnage of that night.

Although the advantages of moving the salient back towards the perimeter were superficially attractive and distanced the enemy, there were many who disagreed with it. Having a wide no-man's land, they reasoned, gave added protection against a sudden assault; the new positions were shallow and gave almost no protection against the enemy who could look right down into them from higher ground.

The failure of BATTLEAXE meant that any further attempt to relieve it would have to wait until the Allies had superiority in tanks and Morshead was told for the first time to be prepared to hold out indefinitely. He was to prepare plans for an evacuation by sea, but nobody except his senior staff was to know of their existence.

The three Commanders-in-Chief, Wavell, Cunningham and Tedder, believed that Tobruk had still to experience a very hard attack, and that the Germans would soon be in a position to launch such an assault. It might well be more than the garrison could withstand and the secret orders for evacuation by sea were to cope with this situation. They calculated that it would take four nights to get the garrison out on warships in an emergency, using many ships, and it would be fraught with danger as soon as the Germans realised what was happening.

Morshead asked for an additional brigade group and more tanks so that he could step up his patrols outside the perimeter, but Auchinleck refused and for the first time as well, ordered him not to go out looking for trouble. When Morshead returned to Tobruk from this conference in Cairo, a series of internal reliefs were taking place. Nobody had mentioned officially that the siege might now drag on without any end in sight, but it was on everybody's lips.

There was no let-up, though, in spite of Auchinleck's caution, in the patrols that went out every night into no-man's land. Seldom would there be less than thirty of them, some of them one- or two-man reconnaissance trips, others big fighting patrols that went deep into enemy territory to carry out sabotage or capture prisoners for interrogation.

They had become a formidable weapon in Morshead's armoury, for they were having a tangible effect on enemy morale. 'They already have a lot of dead and wounded in the 3rd Company,' a captured German diary revealed. 'It is very distressing. In their camp, faces are pale and all eyes downcast. Their nerves are taut to breaking point.'

The bland report on the day after a successful patrol masked the excitement and gore that so often accompanied them. In a typical attack on an enemy strongpoint, a patrol from 2/15th Battalion found itself crawling the last few hundred metres to get into position for the final assault. Suddenly a flare went up and as the Australians threw themselves to the ground, a machine gun opened up on them.

Captain F. L. Bode, the patrol leader, shouted, 'Come on boys, up and at 'em!' and the eleven men charged. Another flare went up behind them and the Italians saw them silhouetted against the light. They swung four machine-guns on to them and a volley of hand grenades burst in their path. For a few seconds they were blinded by the dust and the flash but they kept going.

Something hit Sergeant R. A. Patrick on the helmet and then exploded, knocking him to the ground but not injuring him. 'It was one of the useless Itie money-box types', he explained later. He lay for a moment, temporarily stunned, but conscious of fighting going on all round him, with Tommy guns firing, grenades exploding and everywhere Italians shouting and screaming.

Patrick rolled over and lobbed two grenades into the nearest trench and then ran as fast as he could for the machine-gun post that was at the end of the trench. He reached it, jumped into the pit on top of three Italians, and bayoneted two before his bayonet snapped. He killed the third with his revolver.

Another Italian jumped into the pit and Patrick shot him, too, ripped off his shoulder badges so that the unit could be identified, and then ran for his life towards the wire in front of the post. By sheer luck, he missed his step as he ran over a trip wire and went sprawling. It saved his life. The man next to him stayed on his feet and was shot and mortally wounded.

Patrick took his last two grenades, crawled out through the booby traps, and threw one of them at a machine-gun that was still firing. Then he took cover in a shellhole, waited until it was quiet again and slipped back in through the perimeter.

Captain Bode came in before him with the rest of the patrol. He was singing, 'My eyes are dim, I cannot see. I have not brought my specs with me', and he had apparently been trying to pull two Italians out of a 150 mm-deep weapon pit, in spite of a bullet wound in his hip, when another 'useless Itie grenade' exploded at his feet, temporarily blinding him. A corporal went to his assistance, shot the two Italians and shepherded Bode out of the post. Three of the Australians had been wounded and three were missing.

That patrol had gone out from R41. Another exciting incident happened to a slightly bigger fighting patrol from 'D' Company of the 2/24th Battalion which left R67 at 9.30 p.m. with orders to find a large Italian working party who had been reported to be laying a minefield only 600 m from the perimeter wire.

The patrol were all experienced at marching for long distances in the desert in complete darkness, using only a compass, but it was a spine-chilling experience to be out doing that in a minefield when every step could be your last. They took with them Sergeant Spreadbarrow of the 2/4th Field Company, Royal Australian Engineers, who would lift and disarm any mines they came across and, hopefully, guide the patrol through the minefields.

At first they found no sign of the Italians at the map references which they had been given in their briefing, and they were resting when they suddenly heard the sound of two voices talking softly.

They froze and were just planning an attack on what was almost certainly a listening post protecting the working party, when they themselves were challenged. They didn't hesitate. On one word of command from Lt P. S. Hayman, the patrol leader, they charged the post which consisted mainly of dug-out sangars with roofs made from ground sheets.

They hurled grenades ahead of them, fired their Tommy-guns as though their ammunition would last all night and killed and injured many of the Italians who were shrieking for mercy. The Australians were in no mood to be chivalrous. Then the fighting swung the other way and heavy machine-gun fire began to pour down on the Australians from at least three positions and an anti-tank gun opened up on them. They decided to withdraw, taking some Italians with them.

They had suffered a number of casualties, including Hayman himself, who had been wounded in the back by a grenade. Another lieutenant, J. T. Finlay, had been agonisingly shot in the calves of both legs; two men had eye injuries; and Finlay and Spreadbarrow tried to carry yet another man to safety, after he had been shot in the legs. He was too heavy for them though and they had to leave him. He died later in an Italian hospital. Hayman and Finlay were both awarded the Military Cross and Sergeant Spreadbarrow the Military Medal.

As the garrison's anti-aircraft gunners improved, the enemy changed their pattern of bombing, and night bombing became more frequent. The dive-bombers, in particular, had become increasingly vulnerable as the anti-aircraft guns became more accurate.

Shooting down aeroplanes was still a far from exact science and sufficiently inaccurate for the gunners to welcome the arrival of a new gimmick from the Royal Navy. It consisted of three 20-barrel parachute rocket projectors and each of these rockets contained a parachute which opened over the dive-bombers' likely target, trailing long strands of wire. At the end of each strand was a bomb and the effect on diving aircraft was startling. Some got tied up in the wire, others detonated the bombs and usually went on to crash in the desert or the harbour.

From the start of the siege, one of the weaknesses in the Allies' approach was their persistence with the belief that the infantry and the armour were two separate forces, each fighting their own battle to the exclusion of the other. They did not carry out their reconnaissance together and, time and again, they failed to communicate properly in battle. This weakness was as glaring after four months as it had been in the first week.

An unpleasant addition to the enemy's armoury was a searchlight which did not arrive until mid-July. It was fitted to the back of a tracked vehicle and it resisted all attempts to shoot it out. Patrols that went to destroy it found that it was constantly being moved and they discovered lengths of cable in the sand which appeared to be its power source, which they cut.

The enemy experimented with different coloured screens in front of the light, sometimes bathing the desert in an eerie violet light, sometimes using green or blue. Their concern was to try and find some light that allowed observers to pick up any movement by the Allies, yet did not dazzle their own troops if they inadvertently looked into it. Yellow was used to penetrate the fogs.

About the same time, the Italians began using dogs to warn of an approaching patrol. The dogs were mainly German shepherds (still invariably referred to by the British as Alsatians since World War I) and their barking in the night was an incongruous sound in the middle of the desert.

In June and July the Australian units in the fortress received their first reinforcements. Most of the newcomers were untrained and had never fired a bren-gun or an anti-tank rifle; and conditions for training them once they arrived, were difficult and arduous. But as long as the government was short of man-power with its policy of sending only volunteers abroad to fight, and not conscripts, the problems would remain. They were often so urgently needed at the front that there was no time to give them even basic training in Australia before they were loaded onto a troop-carrier.

The final counter-attack that Morshead would attempt as Fortress Commander took place at the beginning of August. A prisoner who was brought in by a fighting patrol had provided invaluable information about the enemy defences and numbers, and the counter-attack, to be carried out by 24th Brigade, involved attacking both sides of Ras el Medauuar simultaneously by night and capturing R5, 6 and 7 on one side and S6 and 7 on the other.

Not all Morshead's officers agreed privately that this counter-attack should be launched not least because control always seemed to be lost when any attack was launched at night. There also seemed little chance of being able to hold the positions in daylight against a determined enemy counter-attack which would certainly come within hours.

In spite of that, there was better preparation for this operation than for any of the earlier counter-attacks, and there were rehearsals of its various stages. They were severely hindered by Morshead's inability to get any reconnaissance photographs taken from the air. He had now been asking for them for more than three months, without success. Eventually he was told to expect them, but the first attempt to drop them had to be abandoned when the release mechanism on the aircraft failed. When they were at last successfully dropped on the following day, they were found to be photographs of the wrong area.

The enemy had significantly strengthened their defences during the past weeks, working by night as did the Allies to lay down new minefields, construct much stronger sangars for their machine guns and dig a series of holes behind two new barriers of barbed wire. Each of these holes held between two and four troops. The posts themselves, it was learned from the prisoners, were manned by about thirty men and were protected by yet more wire and more mines.

In spite of this formidable strength, the capture of both S6 and S7 was given to just one company led by an old veteran of the Second Afghan War, Lt Col J. E. Lloyd (not to be confused with Morshead's Chief of Staff). They were the same posts that a battalion had failed to take before. No tanks or carriers were to be used initially, so that they could keep the element of surprise until the last minute.

The start time was set at 3.30 a.m. on the morning of 3 August and once again there was a near-disaster before they started. The plan for the capture of S7, the first target, looked straight-forward enough on paper. A platoon, led by Lt S. C. McHenry, was to slip through the wire and, from a position west of the post, give covering fire to the platoon of Lt H. T. Coppock which would go straight up the escarpment to assault S7 at the top. Five minutes before the allotted time, sixty guns of the artillery opened up and the enemy, thoroughly alerted, poured fire down the sloping side of the escarpment, while Coppock tried to advance up it.

As if this wasn't enough, 'jumping-jack' anti-personnel mines burst out of the ground and exploded as they walked on them. Only a handful reached the top, nearly all of them wounded including Coppock himself, and they gave covering fire to the engineers who moved in and blew the wire in front of the post with bangalore torpedoes. The noise was deafening and the stench of explosives filled the night sky.

As the engineers put down their bridges across the anti-tank ditch, Coppock and his three remaining men stormed across, killed four Germans and captured six more, four of them wounded. There seemed to be no one else in the post. It was then Coppock's task to signal by Very light to McHenry's platoon that it was clear to come in, and his engineers would blow a hole in the wire. Instead there was disaster!

Coppock reached behind him for a sack containing the Very cartridges that he had been carrying on his back, but it had gone. It had either fallen off on the strenuous advance up the escarpment or been shot away. Whatever the reason, he was unable to send the signal, and of course there was still no wireless.

He sent out a runner to try and get through to his Company Commander, Captain R. A. E. Conway, but he never arrived. A few other members of Coppock's platoon arrived over the escarpment and were admitted to the post, but while stretcher bearers struggled to drag in the wounded, the enemy could be seen closing in, silhouetted in the light of the flares that lit up the area every few minutes.

Coppock was now wandering around in a daze, wounded and

confused, and he walked out of the post alone telling his platoon that he was going to find Conway.

Left alone in the post, his men waited helplessly for the inevitable enemy counter-attack, but they were leaderless. And then a Lance-Sergeant from the 1/13th Field Company, who had been helping to bring in the wounded, saw their predicament and came back to the post to rally them. He found twelve men of whom only five, including two signallers who had been trying in vain to install a telephone to the post, were fit to fight.

Outside the fence, Lt McHenry waited and waited for the pre-arranged signal from Coppock, but when the first touch of daylight appeared in the sky in front of him, he withdrew his men and reported to Conway that Coppock's mission had failed.

If Coppock had at least succeeded in getting into s7, the platoon attacking s6 had an even grimmer time. Lt J. M. Head managed to reach the escarpment without too many casualties and he was closely followed by a platoon from the 2/48th whose task was to seize weapon pits and sangars east of the water tower near s6. They achieved that objective without much trouble, but it was the last thing that went right.

Head's platoon received an even more punishing hail of fire than Coppock's as they approached. The Germans threw everything at them, from small arms and mortars, to shells and mines. By the time they reached the wire in front of R6, Head had only eight men left and he himself was injured in the neck and legs after walking on a booby-trap. The engineers moved forward to blow the wire and were immediately shot. Head, with no supporting platoon waiting to join him or to give him covering fire, was faced with the certain knowledge that if his men attempted to get through the wire, they would be dead within moments. He did the only reasonable thing and led his men back to the safety of the perimeter; then he too went to report failure to Captain Conway.

Conway, meanwhile, had been waiting at a point called Bare Knoll, midway between s6 and s8. When no signals announced success and nobody came back, he decided to go out himself before dawn to see what the situation was. He set off with his Sergeant-Major and four men and had just left when Coppock arrived. He was still out when McHenry came in, so heard neither story.

Instead, he pressed on and managed to reach s7, though not

without the loss of two of his four men. As soon as he found Australians in possession, he fired the success signal.

Lloyd had waited in his advanced headquarters on top of the escarpment between s12 and s13, which were north of s7. All night he waited for the signal from Coppock and McHenry and, when no word came, he finally reported to Godfrey that both attacks had failed. Godfrey dismissed the tanks which were waiting to consolidate the infantry's successes and they set off on the slow journey back to their own headquarters.

Colonel Windeyer of the 2/48th meanwhile stood down his platoons which were waiting to advance to the new front line that would have been created by the recapture of s6 and s7 and recalled his platoon which had seized the enemy positions near the water tower. As the last of his troops returned to their positions, he could at least be thankful that it was not they who had gone to whatever fate had awaited Coppock and McHenry. And then, quite unmistakeably, high over the escarpment, three Very lights, first a green, then a red, then a green, lit up the sky. Fifteen seconds later, the signal was repeated. Beyond doubt, it meant success at s7.

Lloyd had kept no reserves for his attack and now his carrying parties had been sent away. He borrowed a platoon from a company of the 2/32nd Battalion and ordered bren-gun carriers to take the stores forward. Coppock had come in, but had then wandered off again, apparently shell-shocked. McHenry, however, was still there and Lloyd ordered him to go back to s7 with the others. He set off at once with his platoon sergeant and two other men, carrying more than 2000 rounds of ammunition, and they reached the post safely before daylight.

The platoon from the 2/32nd and the carriers, however, dawdled and then found themselves facing an impenetrable wall of artillery and small-arms fire that prevented them getting over the escarpment. One of the carriers was hit and the stores were dumped in a *wadi*, just 300 m short of s7.

Conway was relieved to see McHenry arrive with the ammunition, but their situation was still critical. They had only nine men who were fit to fight. The engineer, Lance-Sergeant Ross, positioned these nine around the post in locations where they could do the most damage, and he was still completing this task when dawn broke and, with it, the certainty that the Germans would soon launch their counter-attack.

Indeed, even as they glanced out they could see them approaching, seemingly from every direction. The assault came at six o'clock and their fire ricocheted off the concrete and ripped into the sandbags. Unnoticed, sand began to trickle out on to some of the weapons. One of the signallers grabbed a bren-gun, switched to to automatic to fire in bursts, and found that nothing happened. In that short time the sand had fouled up the mechanism.

He picked up a German machine-pistol and the same thing happened and dust trickled out as he tipped it sideways. By now he could see the enemy nearly on top of them and in desperation he grabbed a rifle, prayed, and found that this at least was working. He began to fire. Out of the corner of his eye, he noticed Ross bleeding down the forehead, but it was not deep and Ross apparently went below into the bomb-proof living quarters, dressed it and returned almost at once to continue firing.

Somehow they beat off the Germans and Conway allowed their stretcher bearers to come right up to the post to recover their dead and wounded. Lloyd, however, watching from his advanced headquarters, didn't recognise these gentlemanly touches, which he would have interpreted as a sign of weakness. What he saw through his binoculars was not a brief truce, but the defeat of Conway and McHenry. Then the post disappeared from sight behind a pall of dust and sand.

Godfrey, meanwhile, had sent Lloyd a company from 2/32nd Battalion so that he could continue with his advance if the situation improved at s6 and s7.

While this had been happening on the northern side of Ras el Medauuar, the 2/43rd Battalion had not been inactive round on the south side. Again the enemy seemed to know exactly where they would attack and were waiting for them, and the Australians suffered very heavy losses.

A platoon led by Warrant Officer R. B. Quinn in the assault on R7, went too far in its advance and had to double back, only to find itself silhouetted against the sky by flares. An entire section was wiped out by mortar fire, and the other two sections, having got through the wire around the post, found themselves in a thickly sown minefield. On the far side of this was an anti-tank ditch, but by the time Quinn reached it, he had only seven men left with him.

The ditch turned out to be booby-trapped and though Quinn survived, he now had just three men. He had actually attacked the area where one of the other platoons had been told to make its assault; and this platoon, too, confused by the change of plan, found itself subjected to merciless attack by the enemy. Again the platoon commander survived, but only two others made it back, one of them badly injured. The third platoon, in reserve, was then sent forward and suffered exactly the same fate.

The whole exercise had been an appalling slaughter and sooner or later there had to come a time when the Australian commanders (and Morshead, carrying out the blood-and-thunder instructions of Churchill who never ceased demanding that every last man should lay down his life where he stood, carried the greatest responsibility) stopped squandering Australian lives in this senseless, careless fashion. Not one of the counter-attacks that Morshead ordered was properly planned or properly executed. Yet somehow this blindingly obvious fact became confused with the legend that surrounded the bravery and persistence of men who were sent out on these suicide missions. The siege would have been just as glorious, just as memorable, without this awful indifference to the fate of so many men.

Early next morning, as the dead and dying lay in heaps in places near R7, there occurred one of those incomprehensible moments in war that men of the old school like Colonel Lloyd might have abhorred, but which lifted the battle fleetingly to a very honourable plane.

From both sides, trucks drove out into the bare, exposed sand and began the melancholy task of recovering their wounded and dead. All through the day the work went on. German helped Australian, and Australian helped German as they lifted each other's wounded gently on to their stretchers. The Germans defused their minefield so that the Australian casualties trapped in the middle of it could be brought out, and both sides exchanged their wounded prisoners. In the middle of what only hours before had been a bitter battlefield Germans offered cool water to the Australian stretcher bearers and they worked together until the last casualty had been removed. Then both sides withdrew to their own positions and started killing each other again.

Operation Crusader

Rommel had many detractors in the corridors of Berlin. His penchant for disobeying orders and stretching his resources to the point where he could almost no longer be supplied, was not admired, particularly by the German Army Chief of Staff, General Halder, who constantly strove to clip Rommel's wings. But Rommel emerged unbroken and unchallengeable and he gained even more independence than he had taken for himself before.

All the indications were that he would strike again in force in September, probably mid-September, and this date was in the back of Blamey's and Wavell's minds in all that unfolded.

The Australian government was irrevocably committed to the concept of all AIF troops coming under a single Anzac Command. As far back as 19 April, the then Prime Minister Robert Menzies had told Sir John Dill that it was a matter 'of imperative importance' from Australia's point of view that all Australian forces should be assembled as one corps as soon as possible under the command of Blamey.

Blamey visited Egypt at the end of that month and found Australians scattered among several forces and in ten different areas, so much so that it would be impossible to gather them all together for a considerable time and even then, it would depend largely on the situation in the Middle East.

The 7th Division was at Mersa Matruh in Egypt, less a brigade which was attached to the 9th Division at Tobruk; whilst the 6th Division was still in Crete. There were numerous other detachments and regiments scattered through Cyprus and the Middle East.

There were complications, even if some were more imagined than real, about the new corps, even about calling it the Anzac Corps. The 6th Division and the New Zealand Division had already fought under that name in Greece. When they had been defeated and then disbanded piecemeal, the Anzac Corps, after the briefest of lives, all but ceased to exist. The concern now was that taking the name away from them would be humiliating and unfair when they expected to be re-formed as soon as possible.

Blamey's compromise was to have two corps — the 6th Division and the New Zealanders still belonging to the Anzac Corps, and the rest belonging to a new Australian Corps. This notion was tossed around in Australia and in Blamey's Headquarters and was adopted as a desirable policy, to be implemented as soon as possible. The Australian Government was particularly keen because it had just learned for the first time that the 7th Division's Cavalry Regiment had been moved to Cyprus without any Australian approval and without Blamey himself even knowing about it.

As early as 17 June, Blamey had made a formal request for many of these scattered AIF units to be returned to Australian control, but they did not include any of those serving in Tobruk, which Blamey himself recognised was a very complex issue. By mid-July most of these small units had been relieved.

By mid-July, Blamey was clearly looking for excuses to speed up the amalgamation and to get the Australians out of Tobruk, over which the British were stalling. He found support in his senior medical adviser, Major-General Samuel Burston, who, said Blamey, reminded him that there had been a considerable physical decline in the health of the Australians garrisoning Tobruk. Why Burston should have thought that when the nearest he had been to Tobruk was Cairo, is not clear, but it was exactly the kind of ammunition the Blamey wanted.

When Morshead visited Cairo in the first week of July, Blamey asked him, too, for his opinion on the subject of the men's health and Morshead told him, so Blamey said, that Burston was indeed quite right and that they were becoming too weak to resist a sustained assault.

It seemed a curious back-track when only a few weeks earlier Morshead had written an unsolicited letter to Blamey in which he remarked, 'The men are in good fettle and as eager as ever ... Health is good considering the conditions — a dust storm practically every other day and half a gallon of water a day.' If it wasn't exactly a testimonial to the living conditions in Tobruk, nor was it a letter in which Blamey or anyone else could have found anything to concern them.

Blamey wanted the Australians brought out of Tobruk and he wanted to be their commander. If this was to be done without heavy losses, it should be carried out before there was an imminent danger of an assault. For the present there was a lull in the fighting in Libya. On 18 July he wrote to Auchinleck, who by now had succeeded Wavell, a long memorandum spelling out the requirements of the Australian Government. A copy of the letter went to Menzies.

The first paragraph showed that Blamey intended to rely heavily on Burston's less than professional comments, which seem to have been based on two Australians he met in Cairo who appeared to be underweight.

'1. It is recommended that action be taken forthwith for the relief of the Garrison at Tobruk. These troops have been engaged continuously in operations since March and are therefore well into their fourth month. The strain of continuous operations is showing signs of affecting the troops. The Commander of the Garrison informs me he considers the average loss of weight to be approximately a stone per man.' (That was about as scientific as Burston's comments). 'A senior medical officer, recently down from Tobruk, informs me that in the last few weks there has been a definite decline in the health and resistance of the troops. Recovery from minor wounds and sickness is markedly slower recently.

It may be anticipated that within the next few months a serious attack may be made on the Garrison, and by then at the present rate its capacity for resistance would be very greatly reduced. The casualties have been considerable and cannot be replaced.

It would therefore seem wise to give consideration immediately for their relief by fresh troops and I urge that this be carried out during the present moonless period.'

Elsewhere in the letter, Blamey reminded Auchinleck that the policy agreed on between the two governments was that Australian troops should operate as a single force and that the present lull in the battle made it a good opportunity to put this to rights.

In one respect, had he chosen to use it, Blamey was right. The strain of being locked away in a siege situation; living within sight of the enemy and being constantly bombarded and bombed by him; the boring food and disgusting water; and the heat, the flies, the dust and the sheer boredom that was far more frequently encountered than action and excitement; all conspired to lower morale and produce something very akin to depression. There was, unfortunately, no way that a commander could suggest that his men ought to be relieved because they were getting depressed. Even to hint at it would have been unthinkable.

There was no question but that the general condition of the men was deteriorating, but they weren't on their last legs as Blamey suggested. The recollection of most of those who served there was that it was the wretched, enervating conditions that got them down and made them less effective, not their physical state. What was interesting was that Blamey chose to use this as his main selling point and not the fact that the Australian Government had every right simply to demand that the Australians in Tobruk be relieved and brought out.

They remained, as the German commander of a Lorried Infantry Regiment battalion wrote in a contemporary report, 'extraordinarily tough fighters ... unquestionably superior to the German soldier in the use of individual weapons, especially as snipers; in the use of ground camouflage; in his gift of observation and drawing the correct conclusions from that observation; and in every means of taking us by surprise.' It was not a bad recommendation for a body of men who were in a state of physical decline.

At least no one could dispute that the Australians were in need of a spell and Menzies cabled Churchill direct confirming that he wanted the Australians out of Tobruk as soon as possible. Churchill asked Auchinleck for his comments, but the general was in a cleft stick. He could not ignore the wishes of a Dominion Government which were spelt out so specifically; yet Churchill and the Chiefs of Staff were constantly urging him to get back into battle at the earliest opportunity. The Australians in Tobruk were not just good soldiers, they were the best: they were experienced desert fighters second to none in his command.

On 23 July, Auchinleck was summoned to London by Churchill. He knew that Churchill would urge him to make another attempt at relieving Tobruk in September which was exactly the time when Blamey wanted to take out the Australians. What he did agree to do was accede to Blamey's request that the 18th Brigade be taken out first and this could be done quickly because there was an excellently trained Polish brigade which could step into their shoes. It was already understood that any evacuation of the Australians would involve only manpower and that their equipment and weapons would remain.

It was settled that the Poles would relieve the 18th Brigade during the moonless periods in August and September, with two brigade groups coming out in the first month and two in September. This was later amended so that all the Australians could be taken out in September when greater air protection could be given.

For some reason — perhaps the same reason, whatever that was, which made him overlook warning the Australian Government of the grave danger that Australian troops were facing when Rommel sent them scurrying back to Tobruk — Blamey never told Menzies of these arrangements so that, on 20 July, the Prime Minister had cabled Churchill urging him again to arrange the 'early relief' of the 9th Division.

Blamey was sent a copy of this cable and hastened to reassure Menzies that everything was in hand for a September evacuation and that he been assured of this by Auchinleck and the British Government. What was more, the Secretary for Dominion Affairs, Viscount Cranborne, assured Menzies that Auchinleck had been directed to give full and sympathetic consideration to the Australian Government's request. 'We entirely agree in principle that the AIF should be concentrated into one force as soon as possible and General Auchinleck has undertaken to see to this immediately. He does not anticipate any difficulty except in regard to Tobruk. He is as anxious as you in this connection to relieve the garrison.'

It would be difficult for any normal person reading this to assume anything other than that Auchinleck had been told to speed up the relief of the Australian forces under his command, including those in Tobruk. Nothing was further from the truth.

Morshead was not a party to these exchanges and discussions and had the letter he wrote to Blamey at this time been made public, he would not have been helping his general's cause. 'The troops are in wonderful heart,' he wrote enthusiastically, about three weeks after Blamey had assured the Prime Minister that they were in fact in a state of rapid decline. 'Their morale never higher — the nightly raiding parties and fighting patrols, as well as the daylight carrier sorties, have contributed to this.'

This was in such complete contrast to the true situation, where these were precisely the situations that were proving most irksome and depressing to the men, that it is interesting to wonder whether Morshead was also affected and losing touch with the reality of life in the garrison. Alternatively he perhaps said it because he believed that it was what Blamey wanted to hear and out of a sense of loyalty to his men.

Colonel Lloyd, Morshead's Chief of Staff, went to Cairo to be personally briefed by Auchinleck's staff on the revised arrangements that had been made for the evacuation. He returned and confirmed to Morshead that September and October were now the chosen months and that the 18th Brigade would be the first to leave. Remarkably, there was still not a rumour in the garrison that any evacuation was in the wind.

Morshead, coming in at the end of the arrangements, was concerned and he wrote to Blamey urging him to send the 18th out last, not first, because it was his best brigade. Instead he suggested evacuating the Service Corps and the Pioneers, who had been acting as infantry. This was obviously unacceptable to Blamey, after all his delicate negotiations to have the 18th transferred back to Australian command, but he did agree with Morshead's suggestion that the relief of units like the Pioneers should start earlier. All this was pre-empted, however, by the return of Auchinleck to Cairo from London. He ordered the immediate relief of the 18th Brigade, and with them the 18th (Indian) Cavalry Regiment and some British cavalry by the Poles, and added that this was to take place between 19 and 29 August. His orders reached Tobruk on the 15th.

The 18th Brigade was given duties that would allow it to be

pulled out without too much disruption, and still no word leaked out until an advance party from the Polish Brigade Group arrived in Tobruk on the 20th. By nightfall, there was not a post, no matter how remote, which did not know the news.

Auchinleck had still made no decision on the relief of the 9th Division by the 6th British Division, although this had been approved in principle by the Commanders-in-Chief in London. Blamey attributed the opposition he was meeting to a dislike by Auchinleck and other British commanders of the idea of three Australian Divisions being concentrated under a single command. This may have been a part of it, but a more pressing reason was that neither Churchill nor Auchinleck wanted to see the 9th Division go from Tobruk. Even if remaining there meant a further worsening of their health, they were still tough soldiers who could give good service before they broke down. And most of them anyway believed that Blamey was exaggerating.

The longer the Australians remained there, the more difficult it became to take them out, for the closer the date for Auchinleck's offensive came too. 1 November was the date provisionally set and the 9th Division was a key part of that offensive code-named CRUSADER, which Auchinleck was diligently planning to the last detail. Blamey did not exaggerate when he wrote to Army Minister Percy Spender, 'I am becoming personally the most unpopular man in the Middle East over the matter ... I am pressing this matter again because I am convinced I am right. It is a short-sighted policy, but one that one frequently meets amongst the British, to use up a division until it is worthless for months afterwards.'

Auchinleck sent Churchill a long and frank appraisal of the request for the 9th Division to be withdrawn, conceding that although the health and morale of the Australians was 'very good', their power of endurance probably had been reduced and that he detected 'signs of tiredness in those in responsible positions.' He wasn't specific and he didn't hint at Morshead.

He suggested that instead of relieving the Australians, however, it should be made easier for them to resist by bringing in other reinforcements to fight beside them, particularly tanks. Blamey, in a long commentary on Auchinleck's report, addressed to the Australian Government, demolished most of Auchinleck's arguments one by one. And after two or three months more fighting, he reminded them, the Australians would be quite unfitted to fight again for a long time.

Churchill meanwhile gave Arthur Fadden, who was now Australian Prime Minister (there was no disagreement between the parties on the issue of the relief), a little rhetoric to reinforce his message. It was along the lines that Arthur Fadden should weigh carefully the immense responsibility he would assume before history if he deprived Australia of the glory of holding Tobruk till victory was won which otherwise, by God's help, would be theirs for ever. Fadden was quite unimpressed.

He replied point by point to all the arguments that had been put up to dissuade the Australian Government from calling out their troops, but he did not consider that the military considerations put forward by Auchinleck outweighed the case for evacuation.

Churchill cabled Auchinleck rather petulantly that he was grieved by the Australian attitude but that he had feared for a long time that there might be such a reaction when all the fighting in the Middle East was left to Dominion troops. That had probably never even occurred to any member of the Australian Cabinet, still less to Blamey.

Auchinleck wanted to resign because he looked on it as a vote of no confidence in his leadership by the Australian Government and certainly his advice had been ignored. But nor could the Australian Government overlook the advice of its own Commander-in-Chief. Morshead, who had been able to distance himself from the controversy — indeed, Blamey had ensured that he was kept at a distance by not involving him, because he feared that it would lessen his efficiency as Fortress Commander — stayed cordial with all those senior officers who disagreed with the Australian decision.

There were weeks of intense fighting to follow and many Australians, excited by the idea that at last they were getting out of the fortress, were destined to die and remain for all time under the North African desert sky.

Outposts, with strange names like Plonk and Bash, Jed and Normie, Bondi and Tugun continued to attract fierce attention from the enemy. They were lost, regained and frequently lost again. In time it didn't seem to matter very much. Some of the heaviest air raids that Tobruk had ever encountered took place in September and the enemy artillery took every advantage of the restriction to ten rounds a day that was still placed on the 25-pounders. There were still strange conventions, like the one that made it *de trop* to fire at swimming parties, but one at least was broken by the Australians. For the first time, snipers fired on Sundays.

The relief of the 18th Brigade went on nightly through the moonless period of August. Operation TREACLE, as the Navy called it, required the usual twice-nightly destroyer programme to be increased to four at the height of the relief. The two additional destroyers carried the personnel, while the others continued with the normal delivery of supplies.

On 28 August Tobruk was warned that the moon would soon be coming up and that all destroyer operations would end, for the time being, by the 30th. On that date the last of the 18th Brigade was evacuated. Probably to the last man, they went with a feeling of unreserved delight; it would be later, when there was time to look back and remember the excitement, the friendships, the shared danger, that it would come more into focus. But already they felt that strange bond that would link all men who served in the desert, whatever their nationality.

Morale amongst the 9th Division was not helped by the departure of the 18th Brigade, but there was a lot of fighting to be done and the business of staying alive honed the mind excellently. Yet the rumours persisted that they might be left in Tobruk, and nobody seemed able to give any answers that made sense.

The Australian Government was also not getting very straight answers, although some time would have to pass before they realised the full extent to which Churchill and the British War Cabinet had hood-winked them.

Cranborne, in his telegram to reassure Menzies, was either relaying a directive of which he knew nothing — and he was not a member of the War Cabinet — or he was a knowing party to a deliberate lie. For far from being anxious to bring about the relief as soon as possible and far from working hard to that end, Churchill and Auchinleck had decided that no relief would take place and that they would stall for time for as long as they could.

In a telegram to his Minister of State in Egypt, Churchill gave his assurance that the British Government was as opposed to the relief of the Australians as was Auchinleck. 'Moreover,' he added,

'I particularly stimulated Auchinleck when he was at home not to prejudice defence of Tobruk by making a needless relief.' Both men were agreed that, from their points of view, the relief of the 9th Division was needless.

Auchinleck was determined to keep the Australians there for CRUSADER if he could engineer it and both the other Commanders-in-Chief agreed. The starting date was 1 November and, as far as Auchinleck was concerned, every minute spent on the evacuation was a minute wasted. He did not believe Blamey and Fadden when they kept insisting that the Australians were a spent force, and even if they were tired and jaded, he was sure their experience and knowledge of the ground would more than compensate — at least till BATTLEAXE was over.

He was most concerned that the relieving division which would take over from the Australians, if they left, would only arrive at the end of October which would give them no time to settle in or to rehearse their own part in CRUSADER, which would be starting about a week later. This was important because one of the vital tasks for the garrison would be to fight its way out through the perimeter.

He sought Churchill's help again and Churchill promised that if Auchinleck did not want the 9th replacing, he would 'make it right' with the Australian Government. But Fadden stood as firm as ever and Auchinleck was resigned to effecting the relief.

The first word that further troops would be leaving came on 17 September when the 2/1st Pioneer Battalion and the 24th Brigade, less the 2/43rd Battalion, were warned to be ready to move in the coming moonless period. The Pioneers had been used as an infantry battalion in the western sector and the 2/43rd took over from them.

One of the units which left with the 24th Brigade was the 2/12th Field Regiment, an artillery regiment. They changed places with a regiment of the Royal Artillery which had been based outside Alexandria. When they arrived there they found all the most modern equipment they had been pleading for and which they could have put to such good use in Tobruk, instead of the broken-down makeshift tractors and other material which they had been forced to use. Yet here at Alexandria, it was piled high in the warehouse.

As the Australians went out of Tobruk harbour, they passed lighters loaded with tanks coming in, the reinforcements without which Auchinleck had refused to start CRUSADER in spite of the demands of Churchill.

The sea relief in September was code-named SUPERCHARGE and it took 6000 men out of Tobruk and brought in 6300 without a single incident. The air attack, which had been Cunningham's greatest fear, did not eventuate. And all through the month more tanks arrived.

By the end of September and the conclusion of SUPERCHARGE only two brigades of Australians remained in the fortress, the 16th and the 20th, and there was no secret that in the next moonless period, they would be withdrawn. When the relief was so close to being completed, it seemed almost churlish of Auchinleck and the British Government to still maintain their obsessive desire to delay it in the face of the Australian Government's expressed wish.

It was difficult to see why it mattered so much now, when the relief of all the other Australians had gone so smoothly. Air Marshal Tedder, however, had warned the Chief of the Air Staff at the end of September that although the relief had gone well so far, a major attack by Axis aircraft on the next relief force could jeopardise the whole CRUSADER operation. And if he suffered heavy losses while protecting the relief ships, he would not be able to guarantee air superiority before and during CRUSADER.

That same day, after seeing Tedder's message, Churchill telegraphed Auchinleck that he was going to try once more to persuade the Australian Government 'not to hamper you by pulling out their last two brigades in the October moonless period'.

Churchill immediately telegraphed Fadden and began by expressing the hope that all the troops in Tobruk, whatever their nationality, would be relieved by CRUSADER. He repeated Tedder's warning that air superiority for the whole operation might be put at risk by having to bring out the Australians, but that as it was such a short time until CRUSADER began, anyway, he expected the Australian Government to allow the two brigades to stay in the fortress until then. He concluded, 'We feel that we are entitled to count on Australia to make every sacrifice necessary for the comradeship of the Empire.'

The telegram arrived in Australia on the day that Fadden was replaced by Labor's John Curtin as Prime Minister, but the response that Churchill received showed no change of heart. It went over Fadden's signature and Churchill, not appreciating that Fadden had discussed it first with Curtin, waited for a week before turning his eloquence on the new Prime Minister. 'I will not repeat the arguments I have already used,' he said, 'but will only add that if you felt able to consent, it would not expose your troops to any undue or invidious risks, and would at the same time be taken very kindly as an act of comradeship in the present struggle.'

It availed him nothing and Curtin replied that the Australian War Cabinet did not feel disposed to vary the decision. Auchinleck, for the last time, was told that the remaining Australians must be relieved and then brought Churchill's wrath down on himself by insisting that CRUSADER be postponed for another two weeks until 18 November.

The evacuation of the last two brigades was more complicated than for any of the other Australian units which had already left. Any relief is a dangerous exercise, when units are at their most vulnerable and both brigades were front-line troops so that it would not be easy to spirit them away without the enemy becoming aware of what was happening. Incoming troops normally went into a reserve position to become acclimatised before going to the front, but in this case they would have to go straight into battle. They also always arrived at least one day before the outgoing troops left, so that the numbers available to meet an unexpected attack were maintained.

On the night of 12 October, the first moonless night of the month, three destroyers slipped into Tobruk harbour with 1/Durham Light Infantry and left, without incident, with advanced parties of the 26th Brigade Group.

The arrival of a battalion of light infantry meant that the fortress was now one battalion over strength and the 2/43rd, which had remained behind when the rest of the 26th Brigade had sailed, was free to go. It sailed on the night of 17 October and for the next week there was a constant movement of troops in and out of the harbour area. There was an air of urgency surrounding the activity and people talked in low voices or, better still, didn't talk at all. The harbour was in darkness, the warships shrouded with camouflage netting, and under a brilliantly starry night, a whole ship could be loaded so silently that the sound of waves could be heard gently lapping against the harbour's installations.

The night of 25 October was to be the final act of the withdrawal which had brought such a rift between the two governments. None of this percolated through to the men in the garrison and the respect and friendship between the Britons and Australians remained as strong as ever. There were no emotive scenes as the Australians went, just relief and a lot of laughter that at last they were finally, unbelievably getting out of this hellish place.

Brigadier Murray, the 20th Brigade's commander, said his farewells and at 5 p.m. handed over command of the divisional reserve to the 14th British Brigade. He had just completed this task when bombs began to fall on the harbour. It seemed no heavier than any other afternoon raid, though, and after eating with the British the Australians unconcernedly moved off to find the trucks that would take them for the last time through the bomb-flattened town to the harbour.

Had they thought about it, the men would have reasoned that a much greater threat to their relief than the bombers, was the presence in the eastern Mediterranean of the U-Boats which Hitler had moved from the Atlantic. Their first priority was to end, once and for all, the insolent procession of ships that carried reinforcements and supplies into and out of Tobruk Harbour, with apparent impunity. The U-Boats now sank almost anything that moved at night and they lay just under the surface waiting and watching, sometimes calling in aircraft so as not to betray their own positions.

While the Australians gathered at their trucks, that night's convoy, consisting of the fast minelayer *Latona* and three destroyers, was about 65 km east of Tobruk within sight of the enemy-controlled coast, and heading fast for the fortress. The crews on the ships heard the aircraft approaching, but they hardly registered. Planes were an inescapable hazard of life, but in the dark they seldom troubled them. That night, though, the ships were closer than they liked to be when the moon was up and it was still 90 minutes away from setting. There was enough light on the water to give the men on the bridge visibility, but also to give an enemy pilot a birds-eye view of their silver wake running out behind them. The aircraft came straight in to attack, dropped their deadly load of bombs and secured a direct hit on the *Latona*, which caught fire and then blew up as the flames reached first her cargo of ammunition and then the magazine.

Thirty-one people lost their lives and the destroyers, one of them damaged by a near-miss while taking survivors off the *Latona*, turned about and headed back to Alexandria. The relief of the 978 men, all but ten of them fit, was indefinitely postponed and they made their way glumly to anywhere where they could sleep.

Three days before, Leslie Morshead had said his own farewells to Tobruk and to those who had fought so loyally and bravely under him. His place was to be taken by one of the Australian Army's foremost tacticians, Major-General Ronald Scobie. It was still unacceptable for a Dominion officer to be in command of a division of British troops.

Whatever shortcomings Morshead had in the field, there was no denying that his men had immense respect for him. He had taken over a hotch-potch collection of soldiers, with no loyalty for their new division, often resentful that they had been separated from their old unit, and welded them into a cohesive fighting team for whom the proudest thing they could say was that they fought with the 9th Division under Morshead.

Those who had rankled, knowing that the only reason they were in Tobruk was that nobody wanted to take them to Greece, and those who had arrived ignominiously fleeing from the Germans, knew that they were among the finest fighting solders ever to serve in the Australian Army.

Unforgiving, sometimes unable to see that there might be higher priorities than sending an endless parade of brave men to their deaths for a principle that said you must fight all the time, at all costs; never for one moment doubting that his policy was right; Morshead played a unique role in one of the great campaigns of the Second War.

Perhaps the most touching guide to the respect, almost awe, in which he was held did not come until after he was dead. He died in September, 1959, and as his funeral procession passed through the streets of Sydney, thousands of his old troops lined the way, formed up in their units, medals glinting in the spring sunshine. Eighteen years had passed, but they had not forgotten him.

In the time that he had commanded the garrison, 749 men in the

9th Division alone, without including the Gunners, Cavalrymen, Engineers and all those others who were predominantly British, had lost their lives. Another 1996 had been wounded, many grievously. As one would expect, the 26th Brigade, whose battalions, the 2/23rd, 2/24th and 2/48th and the 2/1st Pioneer, bore the brunt of the attacks, were the greatest sufferers. Their casualties included 249 dead and 397 wounded, a sad toll. How many might have lived with another, less obsessive, commander is idle conjecture.

Churchill was not one who joined in congratulating the Australian Government of the role their men had played in Tobruk. Instead he sent a telegram to Curtin which came quickly to the point. 'Our new fast minelayer, *Latona*, was sunk and the destroyer *Hero* damaged by air attack last night in going to fetch the last 1200 Australians remaining in Tobruk. Providentially, your men were not on board. I do not yet know our casualties.' He added that it would not be possible to resume the evacuation until the next moonless period in November.

Curtin responded equally curtly by pointing out that the Inspector-General Medical Services had visited the 9th Division and confirmed that they had 'suffered a considerable decline in their physical powers.' He reminded Churchill that the Australian Government still expected to see the remainder relieved in the next dark period.

In mid-November, the daring ships of the Inshore Squadron took out all the remaining Australians except for one battalion, the 2/13th, which was to remain. The Inshore Squadron never stopped running while the war continued, but every month the casualties climbed. In November five of her ships were sunk, among them the *Pass of Balmaha* which had brought the fuel to Tobruk when the garrison was down to its last two days' supplies.

The single battalion left behind, the 2/13th, had remained to cover a sector of the perimeter that was due to be taken over by a Polish unit that had been delayed. The Polish unit never came at all and the 2/13th remained. Scobie put it to them that they would only be there for another week, anyway, because CRUSADER would see them leaving the perimeter.

CRUSADER was to be a battle that ranked, as Churchill put it, with Blenheim and Waterloo. For the first time in North Africa the

Allies not only could match the armour and the guns that Rommel could bring against them, but they far surpassed them. They had twice as many tanks and twice as many guns.

Auchinleck's objective was the complete destruction of the enemy's armour, the recapture of the whole of Cyrenaica and, in the course of that, the relief of Tobruk. When the garrison in the fortress was unplugged, Rommel would find a formidable force at his back in addition to the huge army that was preparing to do battle from Egypt.

Rommel's aim was equally uncompromising. He wanted Tobruk seized and, if necessary, laid waste and he wanted Tobruk Harbour. Rid of this troublesome thorn in his side, he could concentrate on his main objective which was to drive through to the Nile Delta.

It was a fierce battle and none suffered so much as the New Zealand Division. In the end, Auchinleck was victorious but it is not really true to say that Tobruk was ever relieved, although 7 December is the accepted day — after 242 days — when the siege ended. Rather the siege was abandoned when Rommel could no longer enforce it. The 2/13th emerged at 7.30 a.m. on 16 December 1941, the last Australians to come out of the fortress that they had fought so hard and for so long to deny to the enemy. They followed the remainder of the relieved troops to Palestine.

On the evening when CRUSADER began, the skies opened over Tobruk and torrential rain, with great claps of thunder and sheets of lightning accompanying it, poured down on the defenders, standing like drowned rats in their positions. Every *wadi* and crawl-trench, weapon-pit and latrine filled up with water like a huge drain. All round the perimeter, flares and rockets were lighting up the sky, triggered by the rain and the rubbish carried along in the debris. It was the first time since the siege began that rain like that had fallen.

The next morning, in that often quite illogical battlefield, soldiers on both sides openly stood up, normally a sure invitation to be shot within seconds. This time, no one bothered to fire. They dried their clothes, made cups of tea and on the German side, even half-heartedly raised white flags instead of returning their fire, when the Poles broke the truce and fired at them.

An Australian infantryman, probably only in his early twenties but looking twice that after six months of exposure to the cruel sun, the dust and the strain, looked across towards the Germans who were suffering in just the same way, and said, to no one in particular, 'Do you know, I don't even dislike the bastards'.

And the man beside him replied, 'Nobody said we couldn't like them, they just said we've got to kill them. All a bit stupid, isn't it? They'll probably say we're heroes if we ever get out of this stinking place. God knows why!'

General Leslie Morshead and Winston Churchill never had any doubts as to why those Australians were heroes. Especially the dead ones.

Bibliography

Carver, Michael, *Tobruk*, Batsford, London, 1964
Lewin, R., *The Life and Death of the Afrika Korps*, Batsford, London, 1977
Liddell Hart, B., *The History of the Second World War*, Cassell, London, 1970
Long, G., *To Benghazi: Australia in the War 1939-45*, Australian War Memorial, Canberra, 1966
Maughan, B., *Tobruk and El Alamein: Australia in the War 1939-45*, Australian War Memorial, Canberra, 1966

Together with the official histories of those units which served at Tobruk and in the Western Desert.

Index

Acroma, 59, 113, 126, 138
Africa Corps, named, 29
Agedabia, 23, 30, 35, 37, 50
Aircraft, 29, 35, 46, 60, 62, 63, 66, 73, 92, 119, 120, 178, 180
Albania, 12
Anzac Corps, 204
Armoured cars, 29, 35, 39, 59, 99
Artillery (see also Bush Artillery), 29, 54, 59, 64, 66, 67, 70, 127, 169, 184, 186
Aston, Cpl F.C., 140
Auchinleck, Sir Claude, 205-210, 212-213
Australian forces, mutual respect for Germans, 10; heroism of, 10; co-operation with British forces, 10, 111; charges of indiscipline and looting, 32-4; described by Rommel, 138; and by German Infantry commander, 206; attitude towards desert, 100-1
Australian units — Divisions: **6th,** 13, 16, 18, 20, 22, 24, 204; **7th,** 16, 18, 19, 57, 58, 76, 203, 204; **8th,** 19, 57; **9th,** 16, 18, 19, 20, 22, 33, 58, 59, 61, 102, 203, 209, 211, 217.
Brigades: **17th,** 24; **18th,** 18, 19, 20, 21, 56, 57, 58, 59, 62, 76, 109, 168, 179, 182, 211; **20th,** 19-20, 22, 24, 33, 59, 110, 174, 190, 215; **24th,** 19, 20, 40, 57, 109, 125, 190, 197, 212; **25th,** 18, 19, 125; **26th,** 19, 20, 59, 179, 182, 214, 217.
Battalions: **2/9th,** 168 et seq, 174, 190; **2/10th,** 125, 160, 165, 168 et seq, 190; **2/12th,** 107, 168 et seq, 190; **2/13th,** 22, 23, 64, 192, 217-8; **2/15th,** 139, 193; **2/17th,** 62, 64, 66, 67-8; **2/23rd,** 129, 165, 176, 184, 217; **2/24th,** 55, 125, 126, 130, 134-5, 157, 160-1, 194, 217; **2/25th,** 125; **2/32nd,** 125, 200-2; **2/43rd,** 68, 102, 176-7, 212, 214; **2/48th,** 55, 59, 66, 107, 109, 113, 115, 126, 157, 160, 164-5, 174, 217.
2/1st Pioneer Battalion, 160, 212, 217

Bagush, 22
Balfe, Capt J.W., 62, 66, 67, 70
Bangalore torpedoes, 131, 134
Barce, 17, 53
Bardia, 13, 14, 20, 51, 122
BATTLEAXE, Operation, 188, 189 et seq, 212
Beda Fomm, 15, 23, 26
Benghazi, 14, 30, 34, 40, 41, 43, 51, 126

Bennett, Major-General Gordon, 21, 24
Beresford-Peirse, General, 119, 121, 180, 182
Bir Ghersa, 190
Blamey, General Sir Thomas, 18, 19-20, 30, 57-8, 76, 203, 205-6
'Blue Line', 107, 124, 126, 160, 165
Bode, Cpl F.L., 194
BREVITY, Operation, 181, 182, 185, 188
Brown, Lt W.F., 176
Buq Buq, 13, 22
Burston, Major-General S., 204-5
'Bush Artillery', 31, 110, 185

Canty, Capt L.G., 129, 138
Capuzzo, Fort, 65, 183
Carrier Hill, 115, 116, 161
Casualties, 172, 175, 216-7
Chakla, 125
Christsen, Sgt J.W., 168
Churchill, Randolph, 190
Churchill, W.S., 14, 29, 39, 42, 48, 50, 118, 122, 173, 181, 187, 188, 190, 202, 206, 209, 211-2, 217, 219
Conway, Capt R.A.E., 198-9
Cook, Lt F.W., 172
Cook, Lt Col T.P., 54
Coppock, Lt H.T., 198-200
Cranborne, Viscount, 207, 211
Crawford, Col J.W., 66-7, 73
Crete, 38, 104, 189, 203
CRUSADER, Operation, 209, 212, 213, 214, 217-8
Curtin, John, 214
Cyrenaica, 12 17, 23, 24, 28, 32, 37-8, 45, 46, 48, 53, 57-8, 64

Dardanelles, 11
Darwin, 41
Deering, Cpl R.T., 139
Derna, 22-3, 32, 51, 188
Desert, conditions, 10, 34, 36, 47, 53, 99, 100-1, 103, 128, 174

Dill, Sir John, 14, 118-9, 187, 203
Dogs, 196
Dummy defences, 38, 120-1
Dunbar, L/Cpl A.E., 63

Ed Duda, 189, 190
Eden, Rt. Hon. Anthony, 42, 48
Edmondson, Cpl J.H., VC, 68
Egypt, 12, 60, 64, 65, 100, 108, 173, 188, 203
El Adem, 51
El Agheila, 14, 30, 34, 37, 38, 44, 109
El Alamein, 22, 36
Evans, Lt Col B., 184

Fadden, Arthur, 210, 212
Fell, Major, 126, 135
Field ambulance, 57
Field, Lt Col J., 169-70
Fifth column, 37-8, 55
Finlay, Lt J.T., 195
Flame throwers, 105-6, 159, 160, 167, 191
Food, 29, 93, 175, 185
Forbes, Capt W., 116
Forbes' Mound, 162, 166
France, 41
Fuka, 22
'Furphy Flyer', 55, 56

Galal, 22
Gambier-Parry, Major-General, 43
Gariboldi, Marshal, 27, 42
Gas, 106
Gazala, 23-4, 36, 59
Gazzard, Cpl L.H., 139-40
Geikie, Lt W.B.A., 71
Gilbraltar, 11, 12, 124
Giarabub, 35, 109
Godfrey, Brig A.H.L., 109-110, 200, 201
Gray, Lt R.J., 159, 160
Graziani, Marshal Rodolfo, 12, 25, 31
Greece, 12, 14, 18, 22, 28, 38, 51, 57, 58, 112, 204, 216

Halder, General Franz, 26
Halfaya, 99, 112, 117, 181, 183
Hayman, Lt P.S., 195
Head, Lt J.M., 199
Health, 29, 101, 103, 204, 205
Heinkel, 22
Hitler, Adolf, 11, 26, 28, 51, 123
Hood, HMS, 187
Hospital ships, 179
Hurricane, 35, 62, 73-4, 119

Indian forces, 42-3, 59, 66, 190, 208
Intelligence, 24, 40, 53, 55, 61, 95, 96, 102, 107, 112, 124, 190

Jeanes, Capt M.R., 176
Jones, Cpl K.S., 159
Junkers, 178

Khamsin, 34, 37, 39, 49, 51, 53, 62, 100, 128
Korizis, Alexandros, 16

Ladybird, 179
Latona, 215-6
Lavarack, Major-General, 49, 57, 58, 59, 62-4, 72, 76, 111
Libya, 11, 22, 32, 53, 57, 182
Lloyd, Col C.E.M., 23, 24, 54, 108-9, 128, 135-6, 168, 208
Lloyd, Lt Col J.E., 197, 200, 201, 202
Long Range Desert Group, 92
Loughrey, Major, 161-2

McElroy, Sgt R., 73
Macfarlane, Lt, 166
McHenry, Lt S.C., 198-200
Mackay, General Sir Iven, 23, 30, 37
Mackell, Lt F.A., 68-70
Mail, 97-8
Malta, 11, 48
Maria Giovanni, HMS, 185
Marsa Brega, 24, 37, 40-1, 45
Martin, Lt Col J.E.G., 57, 168, 170
Mechili, 43, 45, 58, 59, 66, 181
Medical care, 95

Menzies, Robert, 11, 203, 205, 206
Mersa Matruh, 12, 13, 22, 58, 100, 117, 125, 203
Messerschmidt, 29, 35, 178
Metaxas, Ioannis, 14, 16
Mines, 68, 70, 105, 111, 115, 124, 192, 198
Montgomery, General B., 50, 100
Morshead, Major-General Leslie, 20-4, 30, 32, 40, 49, 53, 56, 58, 64, 107, 108, 110, 111, 119, 128, 133-4, 160, 163, 168, 172, 179, 182-7, 192, 197, 202, 204-5, 208, 216, 219
Msus, 41
Murray, Brig J.J., 22, 24, 110, 165, 174, 215

Naval Inshore Squadron, 121-2, 185, 217
Navigation, desert, 99
Neame, General Sir Philip, VC, 17, 23, 31, 32, 38, 40-1, 43
Neumann-Silkow, General Walther, 190
New Zealand forces, 16, 102, 104, 204, 218
Northcott, Major-General John, 20
Noyes, Lt, 171

Oakley, Sgt, 159
O'Connor, Major-General Richard, 13, 14, 43
Olbrich, Col F., 75-6

Palestine, 57, 125
Parachutists, 54, 101
Parramatta, HMAS, 185
Pass of Balmah, 187, 217
Patrick, Sgt R.A., 194
Paulus, General von, 124
Pigeons, 127
Pilastrino, Fort, 67, 125, 133, 165
Pilastrino Ridge, 67, 128
Polish Brigade, 207, 208, 217, 218
Pound, Admiral of the Fleet Sir Dudley, 118

Pratt, Lt L.J., 177
Prisoners, Axis, 13, 14, 15, 51, 54, 61, 75, 111, 113, 116, 117, 126: Allied, 43, 95
Prittwitz, General Heinrich von, 47

Quinn, W.O. R.B., 201

Ras el Madauuar, 51, 52, 115, 126, 127 et seq, 134-5, 136, 140, 157, 161, 162-3, 168, 184, 192, 197
'Red Line' 52, 53, 107, 167, 174
Relief of Tobruk, 203 et seq
Rommel, General Erwin, 9, 15, 25, 26 et seq, 34, 38, 42-3, 47, 49, 50, 58, 60, 62, 68, 70, 75, 94, 100, 103, 106, 108, 112, 117, 121, 124, 130-1, 138, 159, 173, 175, 190, 203, 217
Rosel, Lt J.S., 134
Ross, Lance Sgt, 200
Royal Air Force, 62, 63, 119, 180
Royal Navy (see also Naval Inshore Squadron), 118, 185, 211

Sahara, 11, 53
Salum, 49, 65, 122, 181, 183
Scobie, Major-General R., 216
Searchlights, 196
Security, 40, 96-7
Shelton, Lt J.T., 135-6
Sicily, 11, 35, 54
Sidi Barrani, 12, 13
Sidi Rezegh, 99
Signals, 40, 104-5, 109, 131 et seq, 182
Slater, Brig J.N., 110, 120
Smith, Capt F.M., 121
Spain, 12
Spender, Percy, 209
Spowers, Col Allen, 55, 126, 128, 131, 134
Spreadbarrow, Sgt, 195
Stoke, HMS, 179
Stuka, 29, 66
Sturdee, General, 20, 57

Suez Canal, 11, 12, 22
SUPERCHARGE, Operation, 213
Supplies, 28-9, 100, 185, 186-7, 212

Tanks, 13, 15, 16, 18, 30, 41, 46, 59, 63, 64, 67, 72 et seq, 113, 117, 118-9, 123, 125, 136, 137-8, 140-1, 157 et seq, 171, 178, 184, 190
Telegraphic codes, 97-8
Thompson, Brig L.F., 110
Tobruk, description, 22; fortifications, 51-3; climate, 53; recreation facilities, 92, 174; strategic importance, 48, 108; etc
Tobruk Truth, 55
Tocra, 23
Tovell, Brig R.W., 109, 157, 160, 163, 165
TREACLE, Operation, 211
Tripoli, 15, 17, 24, 28, 30, 48, 121
Tripolitania, 14, 28, 51
Tucker, Capt 161, 163

Verrier, Lt Col A.D., 165-6

Wadi Auda, 54
Wadi Belgassem, 52, 68, 102, 176
Wadi Sehel, 52, 54, 116
Wadi Weddan, 52
Wadi Zeitun, 52, 190
Wavell, General Sir Archibald, 12, 13, 14, 16, 17, 18, 19, 24, 27, 33, 38, 39, 41, 43, 48, 50-1, 56, 57, 64, 67, 76, 106, 108, 111, 117, 125, 182, 187, 190, 203
Western desert, description, 36-7, 53, 54
Williams, Sgt W.H., 54-5
Windeyer, Lt Col V., 115, 116-7, 126, 157-8, 161, 163, 165-6, 200
Woods, Capt, 161-5
Wootten, Brig G., 56, 57, 62, 109, 168 et seq, 179, 180, 181, 182, 190
Wynter, Major-General H.D., 18

For Product Safety Concerns and Information please contact our EU
representative GPSR@taylorandfrancis.com
Taylor & Francis Verlag GmbH, Kaufingerstraße 24, 80331 München, Germany

www.ingramcontent.com/pod-product-compliance
Lightning Source LLC
Chambersburg PA
CBHW070605300426
44113CB00010B/1410